REFLECTIONS ON ROBERTO

By Phil Musick

ISBN 0-9641355-0-7

REFLECTIONS ON ROBERTO

By Phil Musick

In the twenty-second year after his death on a mission of mercy, the memories Roberto Clemente etched in the minds of those who watched him play the game of baseball with uncommon grace and skill have, surprisingly enough, dulled little.

They remain there in memory to be conjured when some moment of true ball yard magic occurs; to serve as a demanding measuring rod for others.

The last great baseball impresario and one of its keenest judges of talent ever, Branch Rickey, liked to apply this standard to a player: "Does he run fast…does he throw hard…does he like to play the game?" Using those criteria and others, Roberto Clemente more than surpassed Rickey's standard.

He was at one with his game. Played it with the abandon it demands at its best, so that no instinctive caution can soil what it might be at its most splendid. Played it out there on what novelist James Lee Burke describes as "the screaming edge", where the games are won or lost and are, in either instance, at their best.

And brought to it a lover's passion.

In The Field:

A line drive glances sharply off the metal mesh screen that rises more than 25 feet above the right-field wall at Forbes Field and ricochets unpredictably. Roberto Clemente is there; regardless of the direction of the carom, he is always there. A bare hand snatches the ball from the air; the throw is an angry, white blur against the sky. Base runners are imperiled. Take an incautiously wide turn at first, be trapped and embarrassed by the throw behind you, as even a Willie Mays was. Be seduced by an inviting base looming in the eye, as dozens and dozens were, and perish.

Routinely, Clemente drifts under a fly ball before it reaches its apex, allows it to fall into the loosely-held glove that awaits upturned at his waist or below. His return throw, insolently casual, is generally underhanded to an infielder, who never has to move to receive it.

AT THE PLATE:

Entry to the batter's box is theater. The back foot scratches for suitable purchase, although not in obvious challenge to the pitcher. A batting helmet is forced down squarely with the flat of a hand, even though it invariably becomes dislodged on the base paths. There is the obligatory repeated rolling of the neck to loosen trapezius muscles, the act exaggerated to suggest they have turned to bronze since he has appeared here last. The bat swung twice, easily but with purpose, the trajectory angled down the way a lumberjack might swing his axe to mark a cut. One bob of the head toward the mound to indicate readiness. And the theater of preparation ends.

Nothing about it indicates the ferocity to follow. The wanton cut of the bat that traces an impossibly wide swath toward the pitch. If it misses, a balletic toe-dance, the protective helmet often spinning wildly in the dirt, Clemente appearing to screw himself into the ground to the ankle. Ah, but when it doesn't, the ball fairly lashed, so that some witnesses instinctively fear for a fielder. Screaming, low-altitude drives that appear like white light and instantly flicker in the power alleys or simply disappear before you're ready for them to be gone.

Each trip to the plate a bit of an adventure.

In Roberto Clemente's day, few professional athletes found it necessary to celebrate their accomplishments with dances, struts, exaggerated arm gestures, preening, prancing, high fives, low fives, or any other sort of gesturing beyond the traditional handshake or pat on the rump. His contemporaries held fast to the belief that such styling in the wake of accomplishment suggests a modest career.

Had their been a baseball equivalent of, say, the spike, Clemente would've doubtless worn his arm out after recording the following high-water marks:

- only the 11th player in major-league history to record 3,000 hits
- first Hispanic player elected to the Hall of Fame
- 12-time National League all-star
- winner of 12 Gold Glove awards
- four National League batting titles
  (missed a fifth in his final at-bat of season)
- National League most valuable player in 1966
- hit more than .300 in 13 different seasons
- had more than 200 hits four times
- hit safely in all 14 World Series games in which he appeared
- World Series MVP in 1971 after batting .414
- led National League outfielders in assists five times
- Pirates' all-time leader in: Games (2,433), at-bats (9,454),
  hits (3,000), singles (2,154), total bases (4,492).

ON THE BASE PATHS:

Always running headlong, straining for the tape. Not a base-stealer in the orthodox sense. But a thief of bases…the ones which are unseen in the record book but are pivotal points in baseball games. The ones born of instinct and a speed gear only engaged when the throw is in the air. The ones which come when a run or its potential are right there for the daring.

Running always with the urgency if not the grace of a frightened deer. If the power of his legs sent clods popping up from behind his spikes, the rest of Clemente was at horrible odds with good form. Arms akimbo, head down and skewed to one side as though the awkward angle might somehow provide one more bit of leverage; bowed legs flailing like those of some berserk old woman fleeing a madman. All appendages alive in different directions at once.

To watch him run was to see a believer fleeing demons. And the slide, his body as flat as a shadow so that dust clouds rose in his wake, motes hanging in the air long after he had arrived at the base and popped up like some mechanical jack-in-the-box, ready to go again.

In most things, on the field and away from it, Roberto Clemente was, well, different. Unorthodox in manner and approach and execution. He did not merely throw the ball; often he flung it the way he had as a boy javelin thrower, winding up with his face in the grass. In his hands, the bat was less probing instrument than scythe and like all great hitters, he met the pitch at the front of the plate and drove it with every last ounce of force he could muster. Catches were not made overhead, but underhanded, suggesting not nonchalance but assurance and singular style, because style was as much a part of his performance as his helmet falling off on that abandoned swing.

The passage of time has stretched or shrunk or warped the legend. And in a place that loves its lore more than most, the legend of Roberto Clemente understandably has been twisted out of proportion and perspective.

He was not the most accomplished player of his time, but only the great Mays truly surpassed him. He was, in almost all respects, a fine man, and that is a loftier legacy than most leave. And the Greeks of Pericles' time would have loved him, for he was, in all instances, true to himself.

This much can be said of Roberto Clemente without fear of contradiction: he was a player of memorable talent and he dredged from it all that was there; he died in the service of others; for a generation, he excited an old baseball town and brought added respect and honor to his craft.

That he came in the fullness of his day to be called The Great One was in no way undeserved or overstated.

21

Before he had been dead 90 days, Roberto Clemente was the first Latin player to be elected to the Baseball Hall of Fame, as the Hall director Kenny Smith had predicted he would be many years before.

"Are you crazy?" Clemente had said when Smith told him he would one day be in the Hall of Fame.

"No," said Smith, "you'll be in here some day."

That day was Aug. 6, 1973, the Baseball Writers Association of America having waived the mandatory five-year waiting rule.

A thoughtful Al Campanis, the Dodger scout who had originally signed him, said: "He will accomplish things because of the way he died that he would not have had he lived."

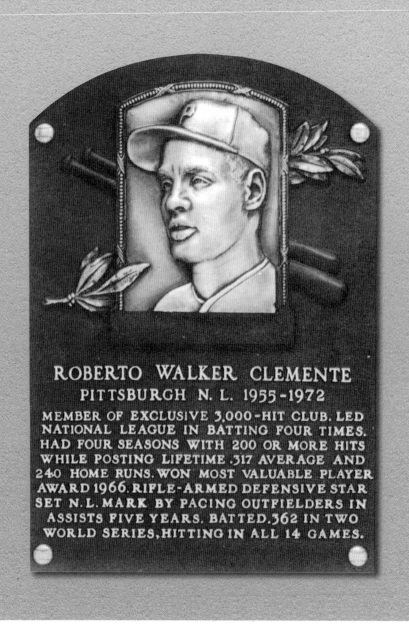

ROBERTO WALKER CLEMENTE
PITTSBURGH N. L. 1955-1972

MEMBER OF EXCLUSIVE 3,000-HIT CLUB. LED
NATIONAL LEAGUE IN BATTING FOUR TIMES.
HAD FOUR SEASONS WITH 200 OR MORE HITS
WHILE POSTING LIFETIME .317 AVERAGE AND
240 HOME RUNS. WON MOST VALUABLE PLAYER
AWARD 1966. RIFLE-ARMED DEFENSIVE STAR
SET N.L. MARK BY PACING OUTFIELDERS IN
ASSISTS FIVE YEARS. BATTED .362 IN TWO
WORLD SERIES, HITTING IN ALL 14 GAMES.

Midsummer, 1970. Wrigley. Batting Practice before a Cubs' game. Noon or so. A day so hot that in the distance beyond the Chicago tenements, the heat seems to gather in columns, like germs in a test tube.

One by one, young Bob Robertson drives batting practice fastballs over the left field fence. Four…five…six. Even the older players stop what they're doing to watch. Seven…eight.

"How you do it, old man," the brash Robertson snickers at a quiet Pirate next to the cage. Soft laughter rises from a nearby gaggle of players, writers and front-office types. Roberto Clemente replies with a stony look.

Robertson hits a ninth consecutive BP home run; then skies the next pitch into a low-hanging cloud over the infield, and gives way to the next hitter, his grin a challenge of sorts. Clemente replaces him in the cage.

Old Frank Oceak, the third-base coach, short-arms a 60 m.p.h. pitch tight on the hands. Clemente turns on it like a snake, catching it fatly and just so on the barrel of the thick-handled bat. It leaves Wrigley on a rising trajectory, as though it had come from the end of a .12 gauge. The ball clears the fence, the high brick wall behind it, and the width of Waveland Avenue, before striking sharply next to a tenement building window.

Clemente flips the bat toward the mound, heel over barrel, purposely ignoring Robertson, and strides briskly off to the dugout. Excited babble trails in his wake. The young Robertson just shakes his head. In the tunnel leading from the dugout to the clubhouse, Clemente permits himself a small smile.

For Roberto Clemente, even on the barrio fields of his youth when the ball was a soup can and the bat a discarded broomstick, hitting was serious business.

Pedro (Pete) Zorilla, the scout who signed him to his first professional contract, liked Clemente's demeanor at the plate. "He always went up there with a purpose," Zorilla said. "You could see it just glancing at him."

More than two decades later, it is not difficult to conjure Clemente at work in the batter's box. The ritual never varied. Approaching the plate, he rolled his neck so thoroughly that often it seemed his head was in danger of toppling from his shoulders. As a teenager returning from a brother's funeral, he had been in an automobile accident that very nearly killed him. The vertebrae in his upper spine defied alignment the rest of his life.

Settled in the box, he would massage a handful of dirt into his broad hands, scatter it, and almost daintily wipe his hands on his pants, the bat propped carefully against an inner thigh. That bit of the ritual concluded, he would look at the pitcher for the first time, nod toward the mound, and take the most casual of practice swings.

Ready, there was no wasted motion. No motion, really. Moving with the pitch, few hitters in the modern era were more unorthodox. Waiting, he looked like a hitting instructor on a video. Head still and perfectly squared to the pitcher. Bat still and perpendicular, left elbow held high. Hands back, wrists cocked, feet spaced nicely the width of his shoulders, hips relaxed and ready to rotate. Deep and way back in the box.

With the pitch, it all went to hell.

As Drysdale noted, Clemente, so far from the plate, looked easy. He appeared to lunge. The backswing seemed far too short and far too rigid to generate any real power. There looked to be a slight hitch as the bat came forward. And as it did, his legs swayed and his knees almost touched. Caught precisely at that moment in freeze-frame, he looked laughably awkward. Fully-unleashed, he was a pitcher's nightmare. The totality, as is said, was more than the sum of the parts. Roberto Clemente hit .317, lifetime.

And he hit them all: the good, the bad, and the waiver wire bait. Noting how far back he stood in the batters' box, some tried to pitch him away with break-ing balls. Better to hand the keys to the hen house to the fox. He feasted on the outside pitch his whole career, probably hitting more than half of his 240 home runs to the opposite field. Other pitchers worked him mostly inside, trying to jam him with the fastball after setting him up with breaking pitches away. The smart ones threw him outside heat. A few tried intimidation…unsuccessfully.

"Some pitchers hated him…Marv Grissom, the Giant reliever, always put the first pitch right there," says former Pirate broadcaster and one-time Clemente teammate Nellie King, waving a hand behind his head.

"I remember one game…Drysdale knocked Clemente flat on his ass in the first inning. He got up and hit a home run to right-center. Third or fourth inning, Drysdale knocks him flat on his ass again. Roberto hit a home run to center.

"Check his record against Drysdale, Koufax, Marichal…all the great ones. He hit them all."

Indeed, he did. As a National League pitcher whose name has been lost over the years once said, "He could hit .299 in an iron lung."

Facing Clemente, every pitcher had a single thought: low, away. Make a mistake and not get the pitch precisely on the corner and at the knees and the ball might wind up among the paying customers.

"There was that one area, at the knees off the outside corner. If you hit that spot with a pitch, he'd look and walk away. If you missed it, he'd hit the ball very hard," Hall of Fame pitcher Tom Seaver told Joseph Durso of the New York Times.

"The very special thing about Roberto physically was his hands. So very powerful. He stood there far away from the plate with that great, big, long bat, and with those strong hands he controlled it like crazy, hitting pitches on the other side of the plate," Seaver said.

This was, of course, a variation on baseball's oldest running gag: Don't walk him but don't give him anything to hit.

"His (Clemente's) weakness was so close to his strength that you were always in danger," said Jim Russo, chief scout for the Baltimore Orioles. "I mean I told our pitchers they could throw low and away, but if they made a mistake, he'd hit it out of sight to right field."

Some of Clemente's brilliance as a hitter has to be ascribed to his instinct for the game and where he was playing it. If he liked to crush the occasional batting practice fastball, and if he chafed any time his power potential was questioned, still he had the will to tailor his style to cavernous Forbes Field, home for 15 of his 18 major-league campaigns.

"When I first saw Forbes Field, I said 'forget about home runs,'" he said. "I was strong, but nobody was that strong."

For all of its beauty—and arguably it was the prettiest setting baseball has ever known—Forbes Field was an architectural mess. Built just after the turn of the century, it was a place of eaves and angles, the outfield walls suddenly changing from brick to iron to brick to wood; all occupational hazards for outfielders.

A 25-foot high scoreboard commanded left field from just outside the foul pole to a point in left-center, just shy of where Maz's 1960 World Series home run destroyed the Yankees.

The outfield wall at Forbes Field was mostly reddish-brown brick, laced with patches of thick ivy. It ran without symmetry in uneven lengths that suddenly switched course like a river maneuvered hither and yon by a shifting glacier. It was 365 feet down the line in left, and 442 at its deepest point in left-center, where it disappeared briefly behind the batting cage, stored there during games.

Re-appearing beyond the cage, the wall ran headlong into another right angle in the deepest point of the park, 457 feet from the plate, before turning toward right field. That broadening expanse was also interrupted. A rippled exit gate made of corrugated iron presided in right, just next to where the grandstand began. There, a green wooden fence topped by a metal screen melded with the bricks, its broad top and bottom molding creating nightmare deflections unsurpassed even by the famed tricky bounces from the right field wall in Brooklyn's old Ebbetts Field.

At various points in Forbes Field it was 365, 442, 457, about 435 and 300 feet from the plate. In short, to baseball parks, it was Yellowstone.

As a rookie in 1955, Roberto Clemente took one long, sobering look at it and forgot about becoming a power hitter. It was simply too big. An unorthodox hitter he may have been; stupid he was not.

"Trying to pull the ball, he might have hit 25-30 home runs every year," former Pirate general manager Joe L. Brown said. "But he never would've been the hitter he was."

Anxious and pressing as a rookie, Clemente hit only .255 his first year, but he tailored his talent to his surroundings, slashing the ball into the spacious power alleys of Forbes Field. Of his 121 hits that year, 39 were for extra bases.

And, when he had fully taken the measure of his surroundings, the swallows did not return to Capistrano any more routinely than he hit .300 or better.

Known in the trade as "a bailout hitter" when he signed to play in the Puerto Rican Winter League, Roberto Clemente owed some of his success at the plate to his first professional manager, Buster Clarkson.

A power-hitting shortstop who drifted through the Negro Leagues for a dozen years, Clarkson was the only manager to ever alter Clemente's batting style.

In spite of the fact that baseball had known a number of successful bailout hitters—legendary home-run hitter Al Simmons comes to mind—Clarkson re-positioned Clemente's front foot to prevent him from dragging it toward third base as he swung.

"Clarkson put a bat behind my left foot to make sure I didn't drag it," Clemente explained. "He helped me as much as anyone. I was just a kid, but he insisted the older players let me take batting practice."

When he signed with Brooklyn, club officials considered tinkering with Clemente's unorthodox batting style but changed their minds.

"We were going to alter his stance," Al Campanis said, "but he kept getting his hits so we decided against it."

ROBERTO CLEMENTE

outfield PITTSBURGH PIRATES

Of all the seasons, baseball is the longest . . . beginning when Winter still owns a harsh grip on most of the country, ending only when the first blush comes to Autumn leaves. If football is a game of frenzied outbursts enfolded in long moments of tedium, and basketball a collision of synapses and unfathomable instincts, baseball commands its practitioners to endless vigil without loss of focus. Across a season that can touch nine months of a year, the imperative is to remain ever alert to the possibilities of the moment without letting your psyche twist your muscles and tendons into clove-hitches. That is what Earl Weaver was seeking to define . . . the ability to remain flexible enough to endure the longest season while not allowing the mind to wander.

That, Roberto Clemente could do. A dervish at the plate, he was all but static afield until circumstances warranted otherwise. Certainly, his defensive style suggested near nonchalance.

Willie Mays made basket catches at the waist; Clemente often took the ball just above the tops of his knees, with a self-assurance bordering on arrogance that suggested it was inconceivable that he would ever drop it.

Other outfielders played the angles meticulously and made accurate throws; Clemente snatched deflecting balls from the outfield walls barehanded and made throws that trapped the breath in your throat.

Many made the occasional diving catch; somewhere there is a picture of Clemente sliding across the rain-soaked turf of Three Rivers Stadium on his knees with streams of water geysering up around him and the ball nestled in his glove.

"He's the only guy who turns the other players on," Pirate announcer and former Pittsburgh pitcher Steve Blass once observed. "Seeing him come dashing in and sliding across the wet turf to make a catch with the spray coming up all around him . . . that's excitement."

Excitement. Is there a player today who can be said to engender excitement? Who stirs the notion that some marvelous play in the field is but a swing away? St. Louis shortstop Ozzie Smith, perhaps. Until recently, anyway. Someone else? Probably not. Roberto Clemente always brought that sense of anticipation to the watchers of baseball.

A man of some wit, who one day decided he preferred the front nine to the dugout and retired to various golf courses while at the height of personal achievement, Earl Weaver offered Roberto Clemente this high praise:

"He plays hard. Once when I was managing in the winter league, he took the first six weeks of the season off. Then, in the first game he plays in, he dives for a ball in the cinders along the right-field line and comes up throwing it to the plate on the money."

Baseball is a hard game. It only looks easy. Far more often than even the most hard-core fans appreciate, winning is the residue of a dozen or more penny-sized moments than of $100 grandiosity. Home runs win some games; hitting the cutoff man and moving the runner over and running out ground balls, and generally busting your butt, win far more.

Aware of that truth, the baseball gods penalize lack of effort. The current players, awash in money and ego, rarely speak of the baseball gods. Nor do the others who transmit the game of baseball to the rest of us. Probably because few deities are as perverse in their sense of humor. The baseball gods, you see, are tricksters. Offend them; the ball takes an impromptu hop at a pivotal juncture or an umpire's view of a slider is distorted by a speck of something in his eye. The baseball gods are offended by anything short of the headlong pursuit of craftsmanship. Or as a forgotten player once noted, "Anytime you don't bust your ass in this game, bad things can happen to you."

Roberto Clemente, particularly afield, did not offend the baseball gods. Old enough for the ballplayers' rest home, he routinely challenged the unyielding parameters of the field: Occasionally even when it made no sense to do so. To understand Clemente the defensive player, and the dominant one of his time, is to understand the relative innocence he brought to the pursuit.

An example. Conventional wisdom holds that the finest catch of Clemente's career occurred in a 1971 game in the Houston Astrodome, about which more in a moment. But another play he made at that site perhaps best explains why he was what he was in the field.

Later in 1971 in Houston, a month or so after The Catch, the Pirates were drubbing the Astros in the gloaming of a game long since decided. With two outs in the Astros' eighth, a right-handed hitter caught a pitch off the end of the bat. A soft fly ball drifted aimlessly, twisting slowly into foul territory. Nothing was at stake save an out that was relatively meaningless. Clemente dashed toward the foul line, legs and arms flailing in a manner that always belied his speed. That he was on a collision course with the wall fronting the stands was clear enough to make the breath catch. He snatched the ball at his waist; hit the wall running flat-out.

Afterward in the clubhouse, the question was obvious: why? Late in a

In his final at-bat as a player, Ted Williams hit a home run. As he trotted down the third-base line, he placed the tip of his right thumb against his nose and as best he could, pointed four fingers in the direction of the Fenway Park press box.

With some justification, Williams hated the Boston sporting press. In the finest tradition of the Boston media, some writers had vilified Williams, who on his last day in the game returned that treatment in kind to those he sneeringly referred to as "the Knights of the Keyboard."

His relationship with the Pittsburgh media somewhat less hostile, Roberto Clemente nevertheless believed that some of his media critics were racist.

That, of course, is a subjective response. What can be said without fear of contradiction is that some clearly seemed to be. More importantly perhaps, there was a racial overtone to much of what was written about Clemente early in his career and, unfortunately, it precluded much reporting on his baseball skills and how they were acquired. The author of this work bears some of that responsibility.

To those who would argue the above points, an anecdote: As late as 1970, there was a Pittsburgh sportswriter who always placed an 'x' next to certain Pirates' names in his scorebook. After lengthy speculation on the reasons for those *Xs*, his colleagues realized they connoted the black Pirates.

Explained one: "He didn't want to make a mistake and cheer for a black guy."

summer during which the Pirates were chasing a pennant, why had a 37-year old player, who just weeks earlier gashed his face making an almost identical catch in a close game, risked serious injury in a game already decided? Had he not risked costing the Pirates a division title?

"What do you mean?" he'd asked that night in Houston, genuinely puzzled why anyone would ask a question with an obvious answer.

A reporter outlined the scenario: He had made a deft catch, but had it been worth the risk? Again, Clemente seemed confused. What did the writer mean? Was he asking why had he challenged the wall in that particular situation? Yes, that was the question.

"I wanted to catch the ball," Clemente explained.

To him, no further explanation was reasonable. He wanted to catch the ball. So he did. It was a matter, his confusion about the question suggested, of the right way to play the game.

Some years later, in a similar situation, Chicago Cub outfielder Andre Dawson would explain why he risked injury: "Because the ball was in play."

John Updike would've understood immediately. Describing Ted Williams' approach to the game, the brilliant author once wrote that Williams "radiated the hard blue glow of purpose." So, too, did Roberto Clemente. And if crashing face-first into a mere slab of brick was the price of playing the game with a glow of any hue at all, so be it.

The particular wall at issue had encountered Clemente once before and he had not blanched on that occasion, either. In some circles in Houston it remains described to this day as "the Clemente catch." Or, as a Houston Chronicle baseball writer referred to it the following morning, "A catch for the ages."

Whatever, Bob Watson—then an Astro outfielder, now the club's general manager—will never forget it. In the eighth inning of a stalemate between the Pirates and the Astros, Watson authored a vicious line drive down the right field line that appeared to be a moth to the flame of a yellow line painted on the Astrodome fence to signify a home run. Flanking the fence at right angles was the brick wall with which Clemente would again become intimate.

Bob Watson was a dead-pull hitter; accordingly, Clemente had shaded him toward center. When the bat met the ball, the sound wasn't unlike the clap of creation. And Clemente sprinted for the corner and leaped. The ball's flight to the yellow line was interrupted by the webbing of Clemente's glove. Clemente's face was interrupted by the wall.

Bob Watson stood frozen at first base . . . staring into the corner with an expression that suggested he was having trouble accepting what he'd just witnessed. He was still standing there, motionless, when applause rolled from the stands in waves, breaking on the distant fences.

"When you get held up by Jesse James, it's not so bad," Watson said later.

An 80-year old retired Texas sportswriter, sitting in a box seat down the right field line from first base, was much more effusive.

"It was the greatest catch I ever saw," he said. "I was sitting maybe 75 feet away and I could almost feel the impact when he hit that wall.

"What guts . . . and to have held the ball."

There are, as they say, horses for courses and Houston seemed always the perfect course for Roberto Clemente, the fielder. It was in that hot Texas town that he once made a play on a . . . bunt. Perhaps coincidentally it was about that time that baseball writers and baseball people (there is a world of difference) began to acknowledge that he was the game's premier outfielder; that not even the great Mays had his range afield or his consistency or his arm. After all, what other outfielder ever . . . ever . . . had thrown a runner out on a bunt?

The victim was one Walter Bonds, remembered only in ignominy. The moment of Walter Bonds' great embarrassment began innocently enough. In an obvious sacrifice situation, the Astros had runners on first and second base. The Pirate counter-strategy—as old as the game but rarely used until the 1960 World Champion Pirates had resurrected it several times in crucial situations—was unorthodox for that time. The third baseman would rush the plate to field the bunt; the shortstop would dash over to cover third, hoping for a force play.

In a manner of speaking, the Astro hitter foiled the tactic, popping his sacrifice bunt into a no-man's land just in front of and to the right-field side of second base. Afraid the ball would be caught, the base runners turned tentative. Walter Bonds, the runner on second, was not tentative enough, as it turned out. Seeing the second baseman had no play, Bonds raced for third. Unfortunately, he had not seen Clemente suddenly appear from right field, skidding across the infield in pursuit of the popup. Retrieving the ball on his hands and knees, Clemente threw Walter Bonds out at third by five feet.

As Dodger broadcaster Vin Scully once observed: "He could make a catch in Massachusetts and throw a runner out in New York."

"No matter what the situation is, we're always aware of what he can do," pitcher Steve Blass had said after the game which made Walter Bonds momentarily famous. "If the other team's got a rally going, he'll make some unreal play to kill it."

Earl Weaver would've loved it.

The throw would come on a line from the deepest right-field corner with hardly any arc, so that some fans in the box seats that jutted almost on to the playing surface would reflexively duck as the ball flew maybe six feet above their heads on its way to third base. Often it arrived on the fly and adventurous base runners would come up out of their slides and dust off their pants and stand, staring, at the author of such a throw. Some would shake their heads, disbelieving.

From the deep right-field corner at Forbes Field, third base was not visible. What guided throws from that point to third was a purely spatial sense, so most right fielders simply threw to the cutoff man. Roberto Clemente did not. The ball would rattle around in that corner and he would grab it and come up throwing, and the box-seat customers would duck and runners would fling themselves at third base in alarm. Many arrived too late.

"He changes the game," Bill Mazeroski once explained. "In almost every one of our games, a runner is afraid to try to go from first to third on a single to right.

"In a year's time, that makes a hell of a difference in how many runs we give up."

Those throws to third base were the measure of arguably the greatest throwing arm the game has known. Clemente made one of them during the 1971 World Series to prevent the game-winning run from scoring. Current Cincinnati manager Davey Johnson, then a second baseman for Baltimore, never forgot it.

"It's got to be the greatest throw I ever saw," Johnson said. "One second he's got his back to the field at the 390 mark, the next instant here comes the throw, on the chalk line."

Strangely, not many outfielders have been singled out for their throwing ability. Rocky Colavito of the Cleveland Indians from the late 1940s until the mid-1950s; Brooklyn Dodger Carl Furillo in the years just before and after World War 2; Mays and Mantle, of course, although neither possessed the lethality of Clemente's arm. A few others, most notably Chicago Cub power-hitter Hank Sauer during Colavito's time. But among the great throwers, only Furillo could legitimately challenge Clemente in terms of both velocity and accuracy. Currently, only Montreal's Larry Walker comes to mind, throwing having become something of a lost art.

Ironically enough, considering he tended to regard them as necessary evils and had problems with most of them, a manager was probably responsible for Clemente's arm becoming the lethal force it did.

In a game at Wrigley Field in 1965, then Pirate manager Harry Walker forced Clemente to understand what a tactical weapon his throwing arm could be.

"He missed throwing a guy out at the plate because he didn't come up on the ball quickly enough," Walker later explained. "I told him, 'if you had charged the ball, he wouldn't have challenged you and you wouldn't have had to make the throw.'"

Roberto Clemente was not a man who embraced criticism, constructive or otherwise, but he accepted Walker's point that his throwing was important to the Pirates in a way other outfielders' arms were not. They had fought before; Clemente had even said publicly that he could not play for Walker. But in this argument, he knew Walker was right.

"The next day, he came up to me and said, 'don't feel bad about yesterday,'" Walker recounted. "'I know you were just doing your job. I play for you. You are the man.'"

If it sounds melodramatic to say that Clemente's arm altered the way the game was played when he was on the field, it is no less true. Baseball is a game of self-evident truths and strategies. Late in games, you play for a tie at home, to win on the road. Two on and nobody out, you push the ball to the right side to advance the runners. You go from first to third on a single to right, and so forth.

Clemente was an exception to the latter truth. If he was in right field, you went to second and no further without studying, as a scholar does a text, the likelihood of safely arriving at third base.

"He changed the way the game was played," Mazeroski said some years after Clemente's death. "Runners didn't routinely go to third with him out there. You think about that a little, you'll see how much that affected games. He saved a lot of runs . . . a lot of runs."

If there is a singular character trait that best described Roberto Clemente it was probably loyalty. To parents, birthplace, the game, old teammates.

During the network television interview following his triumph in the 1971 World Series, Clemente interrupted broadcaster Tony Kubek's first question to speak to his parents back in Puerto Rico. In Spanish, he said: "On this, the proudest day in my life, I ask for your blessing."

Another time he told a reporter: "Someday I will put a sign outside my house and it will read: To God, Mother, Father and baseball."

Each of his children was born in Puerto Rico, Vera Clemente returning to the island for their births at her husband's request.

On the day when Bill Mazeroski was being honored, Clemente momentarily returned to the Pirate clubhouse just before the ceremony. Finding several Pirates playing cards, he said, "I give you bastards four minutes to get outside. They are honoring the greatest second baseman the game has ever known and anyone not out there in four minutes will have to fight me."

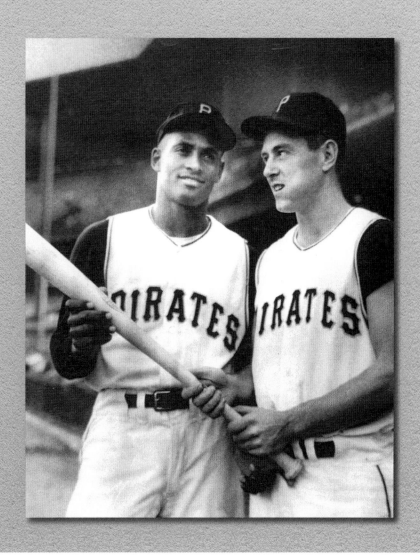

Baseball is said to be a game of inches, but more to the point, it is a game of small increments. Of successfully performing time-honored tasks. Of letting the geometry of the game work on your behalf. Go from first to third on the single to right, your chances of scoring improve exponentially; don't, and so do the odds you will lose a lot of one-run games. As in romance, the little things in baseball count a lot. Or as pitcher-broadcaster Dizzy Dean once observed of a 1-0 game, "It was closer than the score indicated."

Rick Dempsey, who caught for 21 seasons in the majors, once told baseball author George Will: "It (baseball) breaks down to its smallest part. If you take the game like that—one pitch, one hitter, one inning at a time, and then one game at a time—the next thing you know, you look up and you've won."

Clemente's ability to alter the game with his throwing contributed to untold Pirate wins in a way both Dempsey and Dean would've appreciated.

Further testimony to the value of the Clemente arm can be gleaned from his victims who perished not at third base, but at first. Runners with larceny in their hearts but a poor sense of the probable in their heads . . . runners who took turns at first base that proved to be embarrassingly wide. An accurate count was never kept, but surely a dozen or so were victimized by Clemente throwing behind them. And several more were simply gunned out at first on legitimate basehits to right that simply were hit too hard. Among those whose too-wide turns carried them beyond safety can be counted one of the modern era's headiest base runners, Willie Mays.

Fielding a Willie Mays' basehit was cautionary business. Base-stealing was not a Mays art; base-running was. He was this quick: More than once in his career he scored from second on a sacrifice bunt. The slightest of bobbles meant that a Willie Mays in full flight advanced a base. So rarely was Mays challenged that he didn't routinely brake his turn until he had gone some 20 feet toward second base; so respected was his speed that trying to throw behind him was considered foolhardy at best, heresy at worst. In a 1969 game in Pittsburgh, Roberto Clemente fielded a Mays line drive on a single hop, wheeled and rifled the ball to first base. Mays had just about dug his heels in when the ball arrived. He was this badly-fooled: there was no rundown, Mays was tagged out 20 feet beyond the bag by the first baseman.

After the game, Mays, a notorious grouch with reporters, was willing to talk about the play. And he did so with rare candor.

"I didn't think anyone could do that to me," he explained.

Although Roberto Clemente's injuries were numerous—it would be easier to describe those areas of his anatomy that were not unscathed than those that were—his endurance in the game can probably be traced to his determination to overcome them.

For years, Danny Murtaugh dismissed Clemente's back problems as psychosomatic until he suffered similar ailments. By then, Clemente had become expert in manipulating his own back to get relief from the pain. In the clubhouse one day in the late 1960s, Clemente gave his manager a treatment. The back spasms in Murtaugh's back subsided; he never again mentioned Clemente's back.

Elsewhere in baseball, Clemente's endless injuries became a source of some humor:

"The thing about Clemente is that he's the only guy to receive get-well cards after going four-for-five, throwing two runners out at the plate and stealing second standing up." Los Angeles Times sports columnist Jim Murray.

"I think I am the best hitter in baseball...when I am feeling right." Roberto Clemente.

"He could hit .299 in an iron lung." Unidentified National League pitcher.

"My bad shoulder is good, but my good shoulder is bad." Clemente.

"Everytime I hear he has an ache, I expect him to go four-for-four." New York Mets manager Gil Hodges.

Throughout his career, although few knew it, Clemente kept a precise diary detailing his injuries. During the off-season in Puerto Rico, he spent most of his time rehabilitating them.

"In the summer, I play baseball," he once told Pirate broadcaster Nellie King, "In the winter, I work baseball."

BOB'S LUCKY NUMBER IS 3
Roberto tied a N.L. record by getting 3 triple in a game in 1958.

BOB CLEMENTE
of Pittsburgh Pirates
10

HT: 5:11   WT: 175   BATS: Right
THROWS: Right   BORN: August 18, 1934
HOME: Rio Piedras, Puerto Rico

One of the most exciting players in the majors, Roberto led both leagues with his .351 average. A top Pirate since 1955, outfielder tied a World Series rec. '60 by hitting safely in ea. f the 7 games played. Roberto is an expert base-runner.

T.C.G. PRINTED IN U.S.A.

MAJOR LEAGUE BATTING RECORD								
	Games	At Bat	Runs	Hits	2B	3B	HR	RBI	Avg
YEAR	146	572	100	201	30	10	23	89	.351
LIFE	917	3561	474	1062	165	58	65	423	.298

"I've often felt like using a ballplayer's head for fungo practice."

Pirate third-base coach after listening to Clemente's explanation for running through a stop sign at third.

On a baseball field, he ran the way he did most of the things of his life ...with abandon. Someone who knew him well said of Clemente, "ordering his coffee in the morning was an act of passion."

And so he ran passionately, arms and legs flying. At flank speed, he appeared in danger of simply flying apart, appendages exploding off to all compass points. On the bases, he was spraddle-legged, occasionally his knees threatening to bang together. Conjuring him dashing for either ball or base, the temptation is to write that he ran like a girl. But a very fast girl, and one without much discipline.

In the field, though, he had a big cat's grace; only between bases did his form imply desperation, as though something large and quick with big teeth were chasing him. Again, there is a contradiction because if running showed him ungainly, he slid with beauty and skill. Before it was fashionable, Clemente would slide into a base and in the same instant, pop up like some wonderfully flexible jack-in-the-box. And there was no hesitation in the act, nothing disjointed; so that in untrammeled sequence he would be upright, then quickly settling into the basepath dirt, ascending as easily as he descended, and again upright, waving to an umpire for time to brush off the dirt. A single motion, linear and flowing. Ballet on the baselines.

If there was great grace, there was also headlong speed. Yet the hole in his game was running. In a 18-year career, he stole only 83 bases and, as far is known, no one ever asked him why, or indeed broached the subject with him.

Between bases, he was a deer, though, and he was the fastest boy in Puerto Rico when he was in high school. In a 1959 game in Cincinnati he scored from first base on a single to right when Reds' outfielder Wally Post leisurely returned the ball to the cutoff man.

Still, Clemente attempted to steal only when a game was on the line. Reasonable speculation might suggest the fault was lack of instruction. He played fewer than 75 games in the minors and arrival in the major leagues pre-supposes a mastery of the game's fundamentals. Then, there was Clemente's inexplicable over-view of the game itself, which tended toward simplification.

A couple of examples from Clemente's second season in Pittsburgh:

A game late in the season, two gone in the Pirate ninth, score tied. Clemente runs through third-base coach Bobby Bragan's signal to hold up and scores the winning run.

Afterwards, Bragan demands an explanation. He gets one:

"I say to Bobby, 'Get out of the way and I score. If I score, the game is over and we don't have to play any more tonight; if I don't, the score is still tied.'"

Bragan retreats, shaking his head. As other Pirate managers will, he accepts Clemente's unique view of things. Earlier that year, after doubling three times in a game, Clemente bunted with the tying run at second and two out.

Bragan: "How could you do something as dumb as that."

Clemente: "The law of averages was against another double."

If he lacked base-stealing inclination or skills, there was no dearth of enthusiasm for the necessary attempt. Or a close friend back home in Carolina certainly could detect no lack of zeal.

"One off-season at his house, he was telling me about a game that year," recalls Omar Cordeiro. "The Pirates needed a run badly. He was on base and he was explaining what he did."

The explanation required, as it usually did with Clemente, a demonstration.

"He got so enthusiastic," Cordeiro said, "that he stood across from me and showed me how he had slid past the catcher.

"We were on a concrete patio."

"That's how wrapped up he was in baseball. On a concrete patio, he slides."

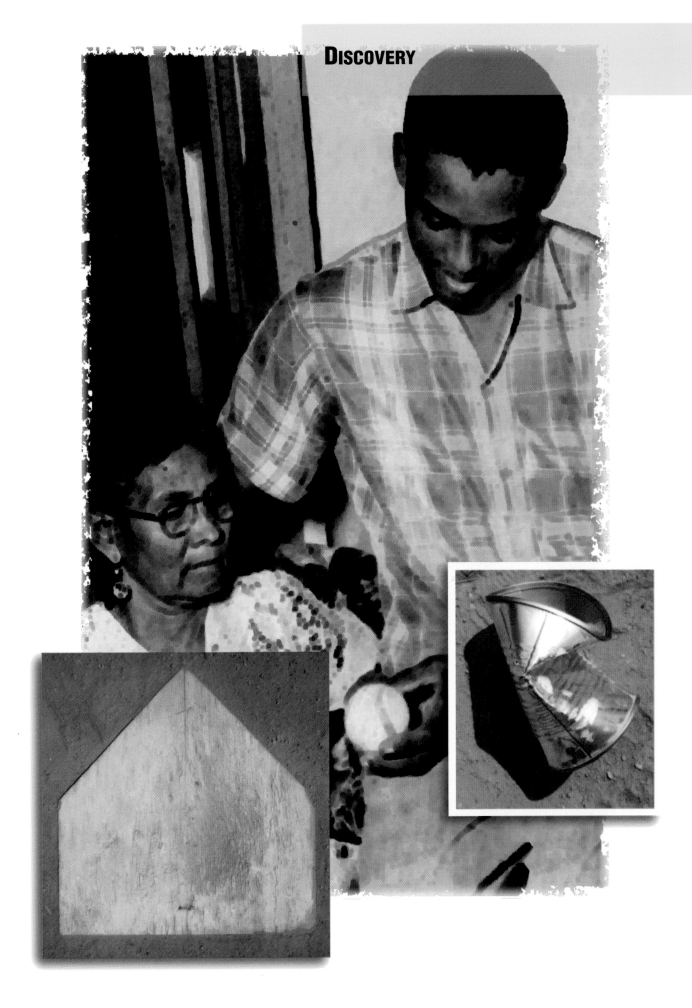

Always, Roberto Marin would study the depth of the dents in the tin cans that flew about the Barrio San Anton ballfields. They spoke to him of strong wrists and shoulders; of future bat speed; of the sharpening batting eye; of kids with the first flickerings of talent who one day might play on manicured fields for money.

Always, Roberto Marin had been a Baseball Man. Oh, he was a son who also dented the tin cans and a rice salesman and a husband and a father. Mostly, though, he was a Baseball Man. One of the legion of Caribbean men for whom baseball is more than an avocation and only marginally-less than a calling. Men with a life-long love of the game who play it as long as they are able and then find ways to cling to it, some as semi-official scouts for major-league clubs. In Puerto Rico—an island 35 miles wide and 100 miles long but with more than a 1000 ballfields—there are a number of such men. Baseball is their passion. Roberto Marin was such a man.

On a barrio sandlot one evening in 1948, while scouting talent for a team his company sponsored in a Class A slowpitch softball league in San Juan, Marin discovered Roberto Clemente, slasher of tin cans nonpareil.

"The way they would play, one player bats, the rest field," Marin said. "If you strike out, you have to pitch. I see this one kid…he never strike out. Bam! Bam! Bam! Tin cans all over the field!

"I say, 'who are you?' He says, 'I am Momen.'"

From his earliest days in a neat white frame house set in a grove of banana trees in San Anton, Roberto Clemente was called Momen. No one could ever recall precisely who gave him the nickname.

Clemente's parents (above) and Clemente family gathering

ing if not serious. His life, early and late, was governed by Jibaro principles and they command a sober view of life.

Strictly defined, the Jibaro culture belongs to Puerto Rico's mountainous tropical interior, but it long ago found its way to the island's coastal regions, where its tenets took root.

"Roberto thought very well of the Jibaros," said his attorney and close friend, Elfren Bernier. "They are a quiet people...very close to their families. They give to each other. He was like that."

Work is a Jibaro virtue much like gambling is a Pete Rose vice. So, from age eight, Roberto Clemente often worked the cane with his father and four older brothers.

"They were poor, the Clementes ...almost dirt poor," said an old family friend. "But they were hard-working, cultured people. Not sophisticated, just good people who did right by others."

Life for young Roberto Clemente, then, became work and baseball. Or, for a couple of years, baseball and softball, his first love as a teenager. Understand, softball, slow pitch or fast, has always been a passion of San Juan fans. It wasn't, and still isn't, unusual for a high-caliber game to draw hundreds of fans.

When Clemente was 14, the softball team sponsored by Roberto Marin's Sello Roja Rice Company moved into a first-rank fast pitch league and Clemente became the darling of San Juan crowds. But the transition from lobbed tin cans to rising fastballs was a difficult one. Young Roberto Clemente couldn't hit worth a lick.

"He was an outstanding shortstop, but we batted him eighth," said Juan Perez, a Carolina used-car dealer who oversaw the team that Marin managed. "We played under the lights and he didn't hit well, but he made sensational plays in the field, and his cap would fall off and the people loved him."

His father, Melchor, worked in the cane fields as a supervisor and ran a small groceria; his mother, Luisa, raised seven children and laundered the clothing of the sugar barons. Clemente family life was lived out according to some self-evident truths: You worked hard; you got what education you could; you accepted that life was hard; you paid your debts; you accorded and demanded respect; you assisted the less fortunate.

The Clementes, all of them, were serious business. Melchor Clemente was as straight and lean and hard as a machete, and the color of burnished copper. When he was into his 90s, on the 1970 night at Three Rivers Stadium when Pittsburgh honored his son, Melchor Clemente still retained the look of aguioso. Pride. Someone there said, "Clemente's father looks like a tired eagle."

The son, too, was marked by aguioso. And he got his marching orders early. "I want you to be a good man...a serious man," Melchor Clemente told his youngest son well before he went to school.

Perhaps nothing in his later life so marked Roberto Clemente than that simple admonition. The manner of his death proved his goodness, and he was noth-

In short order, though, the Clemente batting eye and stroke improved and the baseball men of Puerto Rico began taking note.

At 15, Clemente was chosen to play in a San Juan youth league program for "future stars." At 16, he was a district all-star for Julio Vizcarrando High School and played for Ferdinand Juncos in a Puerto Rican amateur league the equivalent of the lower minors in this country. And, God, could he throw. In high school, he threw the javelin 190 feet and there was talk he would compete for Puerto Rico in the 1952 Olympic Games at Helsinki. In retrospect, the arm was something of a legacy, inherited from Luisa Clemente.

"My arm is the same shape as my mother's," Clemente explained. "When she was 75, she threw out the first pitch to start the winter league season. And she had something on it."

During Roberto Clemente's 17th summer, his latent talent for the game came into full blossom. Still the wild swinger he would remain for several years, he began to make better contact and started to show signs of strength. A gap hitter, mostly to the right side, he displayed the power as he got bigger. And, importantly to Roberto Marin, he began to pull the ball with authority. The foot speed was there—early that summer Clemente had beaten the island's best schoolboy 440 runner in a festival meet. About the arm, there was no question. The previous winter, Marin had studied the professionals of the Puerto Rican Winter League; in his mind, Clemente compared favorably with them. In July, Marin decided: It was time for Clemente to meet the island's best-known Baseball Men.

"I told him that to me he looked better than the professional outfielders here in the winter league," Marin said. "I told him I was going to take him to a tryout that a Brooklyn Dodger scout was going to hold in Santurce."

You would've been hard-pressed to distinguish whether Roberto Clemente took more pride in Puerto Rico, or it in him. Alive, he never failed to use his celebrity to celebrate the place of his birth; dead, he served it as an eminently-worthy symbol of its virtues, glories and passions .

As another distinguished Puerto Rican, actor Jose Ferrer, put it so well: "It is said that the death of any man diminishes us all… that is particularly true of good men."

The youngest of five sons of Melchor and Luisa Clemente, Roberto was born and raised in Carolina, a town of about 15,000 near the capital of San Juan in the Northeast quadrant of he rectangular-shaped island.

A U.S. commonwealth, Puerto Rico's 3.5 million population is largely located in its coastal cities, valleys and lowlands. More than 70 percent of the population is urban. The lush interior of the island is mountainous.

Contrary to popular belief, Puerto Rico is highly-industrial and its annual exports of medicine, machinery, scientific instruments, and plastic, glass and fabricated metal products exceed $25 billion.

One hundred miles long and 35 miles wide, it is arguably the baseball capital of Latin America, with more than 1000 fields. Baseball is a Puerto Rican passion.

"Every boy has his hero," Ferrer noted in a video on Clemente's life produced by major-league baseball. "And in Puerto Rico, that hero is Roberto Clemente."

"I couldn't believe my eyes."

Brooklyn Dodger scout Al Campanis, watching 17-year old Roberto Clemente throw and run.

Tryout camps are now largely a relic of the game, consigned to dusty memory along with uniform pants worn just below the knee, crackerjack instead of nachos, and pivot men with scarred legs. Once, though, they were the stuff of many dreams: Grouchy old scouts with stopwatches and cigars and wise eyes that spoke of small expectations. Nervous kids from farms and midland villages and factories and Latin scrub lots. The search in those times was for that one kid who would fit the late Branch Rickey's twangy standard: Did he run fast…did he throw hard…did he like to play the game?

On a thousand fields, Al Campanis, a seer of unripened talent, looked for such a kid. Once he found a wild left-hander named Sandy Koufax. Mostly, though, the kids are suspects not prospects. Come to a tryout camp hoping against hope. Knowing the long odds. Armed with only ambition and talent that loomed large in Peoria, only to shrink under a professional gaze. Occasionally there were unpolished jewels. A Koufax, heat fairly blazing from an uncontrollable fastball. A Mantle, driving the ball out of sight into the dusty Oklahoma afternoon. A Clemente.

Baseball's color line breached by Brooklyn Dodger boss Rickey and Jackie Robinson in 1947, the following spring found a dozen clubs scratching at the barely-tapped Caribbean motherlode. The Washington Senators were first; Rickey determined the Dodgers would dig deeper. Al Campanis—some 40 years later to be drummed out of the game as a Dodger vice president for imprudent racial remarks—was his shovel.

By 1952, the affable Campanis had become established as a Caribbean scout; knew the Roberto Marins of Puerto Rico. That summer he would uncover a jewel named Clemente. But Campanis tells it best:

"I had done one of those camps a year or two before down in Aguadilla. Nothing. Then in '52, I held one in San-

turce at Sixto Escobar Stadium. Maybe 70 kids…72, I think.

"I lined them up in centerfield and told them to throw to the plate. Lot of arc on the throws. Then one kid throws a bullet, on the fly. I shouted 'uno mas!' Again, a bullet. I couldn't believe my eyes. I said, 'That's all.'

"Hell, you can't gild a lily.

"After that, I timed them in the 60-yard dash. This kid runs it in 6.4. I said 'uno mas!' Another 6.4. In a baseball uniform yet. Hell, the world's record then was only 6.1.

"I couldn't believe it.

"Clemente gets in the cage and I noticed how far he stood from the plate. I had a minor-league pitcher there, Pantalone Santiago, and I told him to keep the ball outside.

"Shots! He hit line drives all over the place while I'm behind the cage telling myself we got to sign him if he can just hold the bat in his hands.

"How could I miss him? He was the greatest natural athlete I ever saw as a free agent."

Still, there was a problem. Roberto Clemente was only 17; baseball law then prohibited him from being signed until he was 18. Campanis would wait.

Pedro Zorilla would not. Chief Caribbean scout for the New York Giants, who would later export Orlando Cepeda and Reuben Gomez to the majors, he operated the Santurce Crabbers of the Puerto Rican Winter League. The day after the Dodger tryout camp, Marin told Zorilla where he could see Clemente play. Zorilla watched one game—Clemente doubled twice, tripled and cut down the potential winning run at the plate in the ninth—and signed him to a Santurce contract for a $450 bonus and "$45 a week to learn to wear a uniform."

Marin to Campanis to Zorilla…one of scouting's finest double play combinations, as it turned out. Marin, a friend who would be in his home the night of Clemente's death, had steered a precise

Dodger great Jim (Junior) Gilliam and a young Clemente.

course. Campanis would later be critical to the young professional's career. Zorilla, wise in baseball's ways, saw to the further blossoming of a special talent.

Baseball annals, though, are awash with special talents, ruinously exposed to their shortcomings far too soon. Beautiful flowers wilted in the crucible's heat. In Roberto Clemente's first professional season, he batted 77 times in 70 games and was held out of the Caribbean World Series. He never quite forgave Zorilla for that, but he should have.

"I never let the young ones play much," Zorilla said years later. "We had great pitchers here in the winter league. Satchel Paige, pitchers like that. The ball comes to the plate looking like an aspirin tablet. A young boy like Clemente strikes out three, four times a couple of games in a row, he starts asking questions of himself: 'Can I hit? Can I really play?'

"It is important he does not give himself the wrong answers."

Under Zorilla's tutelage, Clemente gave himself few wrong answers. But when owner Horace Stoneham refused his scout's strong suggestion that the Giants sign Clemente, saying "he strikes out too much," Zorilla called Al Campanis. The Dodger scout well remembered the dusty tryout camp field.

Zorilla roughed out an informal agreement with Brooklyn on a West Indies Cable & Telegraph Ltd. telegram blank. The Dodgers offered Clemente a $10,000 signing bonus—big money then—and a $5000 salary for the 1954 season. The baseball gods secretly smiled on the Pittsburgh Pirates. Ironically, Rickey would be running the club 18 months later.

Within two weeks, nine clubs had contacted Clemente and the Milwaukee Braves upped their bonus offer to $25,000. Having given his word to Campanis, Clemente signed with the Dodgers. They wouldn't have him for long.

ROBERTO WALKER CLEMENTE

outfield Pittsburgh Pirates

Roberto was the Pirates' 1st choice at the 1954 Winter Draft. Originally signed by the Dodgers to a bonus contract, he showed his powerful throwing arm and extra base hitting ability at Montreal last year. During the Winter, Roberto played in the Puerto Rican League and placed 2nd in hitting. His 73 hits at Santurce gave him a glittering .365 Batting Average.

Height: 5-11
Weight: 175
Bats: Right
Throws: Right
Home:
Carolina, P. R.
Born:
Aug. 18, 1934

In reflection, anger seemed to be the fuel that drove him headlong in the pursuit of greatness. But not a singular anger, directed at one source of his rage. Anger at bigotry…anger at mere unfortunate circumstance…anger at his own youthful fallabilities…anger at insults, real and imagined…anger at being misunderstood…and, most importantly, anger nurtured and stoked for a purpose.

Roy McHugh, the Pittsburgh Press wordsmith, put it best once late in Roberto Clemente's career when he again lashed out at the sporting press: "He's revving himself up to win another batting title."

Rage released seemed to race the Clemente engine. It began to percolate in 1954 when the Dodgers sent him to Montreal of the International League in a failed attempt to hide him lest he be lost in the winter draft. And, indeed, it was still boiling over when it was a factor in bringing about his death two decades later. Always he seemed baseball's last angry man...trying, as the Man of La Mancha did, to right the unrightable wrong. As well, of course, as trying to reach the unreachable star.

Clemente admitted as much.

"If I am not angry," he said one day in 1969, "I am not as good a ballplayer."

Perhaps he even sensed that as a rookie with Montreal; not that his treatment there grated any less. If Brooklyn coveted the young Clemente, still the Dodgers were in a quandary. On a big-league club with an outfield boasting Duke Snider, Carl Furillo and Jackie Robinson, there was simply no room for the 19-year old Clemente in Flatbush, so he was secreted off to Montreal to be played only sparingly in the hope no other club would notice him.

Clemente seethed.

His first week with the Royals, he hit a home run into a stiff wind that exited from a spot in Delerimier Stadium that no Royal in history had reached; the next day he was benched. The season played out that way. Weekly, he threatened to quit.

Joe Black, later to become a pitching mainstay in Brooklyn and a high-ranking official with Greyhound, was a teammate of Clemente's that summer.

"His inner drive wasn't being satisfied," Black said, "and it was very frustrating for him. He had it and he knew he had it, and he just couldn't understand why he wasn't playing."

Moreover, speaking neither English nor French, Clemente simply couldn't understand much of anything. One night a Toronto player he had robbed of a home run—becoming snagged atop the fence by his belt and having to be extricated by the ground crew—called him a son of a bitch. Clemente replied: "Thank you."

Told of the insult, a burgeoning pride inspired Clemente to return it threefold. "Son of a bitch…son of a bitch…son of a bitch," he screamed at the Toronto offender. But unfamiliarity with the language made him embarrassed and angrier. The word "nigger" wasn't socially unacceptable in 1954; Clemente heard it a lot. And would continue to. But not in Montreal.

Had Roberto Clemente been aware of Clyde Sukeforth, his anger probably would've abated. That June, in Montreal to scout Joe Black for a possible trade, Pirate scout Sukeforth spotted Clemente. Mesmerized, he watched him throw and hit in a pre-game workout. The woebegone Pirates would make the first selection in the coming winter draft. After the game, in which Clemente did not play, Sukeforth sidled up to Montreal manager Max Macon.

"Take care of our boy, Max," Sukeforth said with a grin. "Make sure nothing happens to him."

Something did several months later; the Pirates drafted Clemente off the Montreal roster, incidentally costing Brooklyn the largest bonus it had paid a player since Jackie Robinson seven years before.

But if life in Montreal had built a fire in him, in Pittsburgh the next two summers, it would become a conflagration. Clemente's war had multiple fronts: teammates who thought him a malingerer; the press who thought him, as one wrote, "a Puerto Rican hot dog"; a multitude of redneck bench jockeys; and those who made him fully aware that he was Latin and black and different.

It was being different—at home, they fried bananas, here they put them on Wheaties—that fueled the him. And often made him melancholy.

Once asked why he was so patient with autograph seekers, he said plaintively, "I was lonely . . . I had nothing else to do. I couldn't speak English . . . that is a terrible problem.

"Not to speak the language meant you were different."

Indeed, some years later after he had become established in Pittsburgh, a woman asked Clemente if he wore a loincloth back in Puerto Rico. "Some people act as though they think I lived in a jungle," he sighed.

As Orlando Cepeda put it: "It took guts for us just to come here."

In dugouts during rain delays, in buses from airports to hotels, in clubhouses when playing cards palls and time crawls on its hands and knees, the men who now run the games but a generation before played them, still make the comparisons. Mays vs. Mantle . . . Mantle vs. Williams... Ruth vs. Aaron... Aaron vs. Joe D. And around the National League amongst those with tobacco-stained teeth, Mays vs. Clemente.

What doesn't get talked about much is the influence Mays had over the younger Clemente. It was considerable in 1954 when Mays—who led the National League with a .345 average that season and made arguably baseball's best-known catch off Vic Wertz in the World Series—joined a young Clemente on the Santurce team in the Puerto Rican Winter League.

Both hit better than .400 that winter and Roberto Marin, the barrio scout, later said: "That was Roberto's big break, playing next to Mays. He watched Mays like a hawk, used to talk about how he played. Mays... told him how to charge the ball, told him not to worry about gambling on a catch at his ankles because in the major leagues other outfielders would back him up."

But, according to Clemente and baseball historians, Mays did not teach Clemente the basket catch both used throughout their careers.

Despite baseball's conventional wisdom, neither Mays nor Clemente invented catching the ball at the waist, or in Clemente's case at mid-thigh.

Clemente always insisted he had caught the ball that way as a young softball player and that Puerto Rican outfielder Luis Olmo had used the basket catch.

In fact, the point was moot. Years before Olmo or Mays or Clemente, Giant infielder and later major-league manager Bill Rigney was said by baseball historians to have been the first player to routinely use the basket catch earlier.

The Clemente apprenticeship was, as they usually are in baseball, as difficult on the field as off. Forbes Field was gargantuan—457 feet from the plate at one point in left-center field. In The Show, as they say, pitchers exploited his tendency to swing at anything visible and the fact that he stood so deep in the box and far from the plate. The language barrier prevented him from explaining that he missed a number of games his first and third seasons because he had been badly-injured in an accident. Returning from a brother's funeral following the 1954 winter league season, Clemente's car had been struck broadside at a San Juan intersection by an automobile traveling 60 miles per hour. The crash—the other driver was drunk—dislodged spinal disks and back ailments plagued Clemente the rest of his life. His teammates, mostly a motley collection of castoffs and poseurs, and the press were unimpressed. Both rode him without conscience.

"Why?" Clemente asked confidant Phil Dorsey, a local postal worker. "I never hurt anyone in my whole life."

Ignorance is the only explanation for the treatment he received from much of the Pittsburgh media, not a member of which could speak a word of Spanish. Other, of course, than "Puerto Rican hot dog."

"Why the hell they picked on a kid who hadn't ever played before is beyond me," former Pirate general manager Joe L. Brown said years later. "The trouble was that he was driven, and anyone who is different was automatically wrong."

In short order during his rookie season, anger turned Clemente's pride stiff-necked. But, even then, it was still fuel. If he only hit .255 his first year, in 1956 he was hitting .350 in late June and finished at .311.

"He began to get used to things, people," Dorsey said.

Bill Virdon, a Clemente teammate in 1956 who later managed the club and is currently a Pirate coach, and Dale Long, who that year set a record with home runs in eight consecutive games, helped. The number of battered batting helmets dwindled.

"Dale was very helpful to him," a player from the 1956 club said. "He was sympathetic and he could kid him the right way . . . get him to open up."

Malingering, in the peculiar vernacular of baseball, is referred to as "jaking." In 1956, Clemente could no longer be accused of jaking, playing in 147 games despite injuries. If he remained angry, if that anger was high-octane stuff as McHugh later theorized, then in two summers Roberto Clemente stepped to the precipice of stardom.

"He knew he was going to make it," Virdon said. "He didn't even think about not making it."

Still, the anger bubbled beneath the surface, although Clemente seemingly became aware of its value.

"If I would be happy, I would be a bad ballplayer," he said after his apprenticeship was completed. "With me, when I get mad, it puts energy into my body."

The greatest outfield in the history of baseball . . . owner Horace Stoneham came within about the thickness of this page of putting it in the livery of his New York Giants: Roberto Clemente, Willie Mays and Henry Aaron.

The Giants had the first crack at all three, but signed only Mays. Stoneham thought Clemente "struck out too much" and Aaron's habit of hitting cross-handed in the minors was said to have put him off.

Had all three played with the Giants, only the imagination might've placed constraints on their collective accomplishments. Defensively, they would have had few shortcomings. Even Aaron, the least accomplished among them as an outfielder, had one of the most lethal throwing arms of his day.

For the record, Clemente, Mays and Aaron would've combined for: seven batting titles, 46 all-star appearances, 1645 home runs, four MVP awards, led the National League in RBI on four occasions, hit for a combined career average of .308, and won 24 Gold Gloves and seven home-run titles.

I see things I have conjured in my imagination and my memory over a long period of time. Then it just all pours out." Vincent Van Gogh said, when asked how he painted.

Joe Garagiola, who turned a boyhood at Yogi Berra's elbow into a show business career, once wrote a book called "Baseball Is A Funny Game." For Garagiola, perhaps it was. He hit .257, lifetime.

For Roberto Clemente, it was anything but. And Stargell's sentiment aside, for Clemente baseball was work. Not drudgery, you understand. Not swinging a pick, or cutting cane, or baking your brain 20 feet in front of a blast furnace. Still, work. And, as he came of age in the last few years of the 1950s to stand just shy of superstar status, the equipment necessary to perform that work began to balk.

The spinal disk jolted loose by the automobile accident after his brother Osvaldo's funeral floated with a random meanness. Indeed, just before going to training camp in 1956, Clemente told his mother and father, "I will try it for one more year… if I still hurt, then I will quit."

One season, a shoulder went lame just after the all-star game. Another year, he was hit on the elbow by a pitch less than 30 days into the season and returned to the lineup in July only to be plagued by bone chips throughout the remainder of the season. Hell, one summer he went to a doctor because of the recurring back ailment, only to be told his tonsils were inflamed and would have to be removed. At times, he had insomnia.

And through it all in those crucible summers leading up to the Pirates' World Series championship in 1960 and his rise to preeminence as a player, Roberto Clemente began living out his fantasies in the way boys have done from the time of the first bat and ball, and in the manner professional athletes now do routinely.

The practice is known as "visualization" and the result, documented by research in recent years, is what is known as "muscle memory." Among its chief advocates these days are San Diego outfielder Tony Gwynn; retired New York Giant linebacker Lawrence Taylor, now using it exclusively to improve his putting; and professional golfers too numerous to mention.

It is supremely ironic that in Clemente's case, for a long time visualization was attributed to laziness.

Before games, he would lay on the rubdown table in trainer Tony Bartirome's quarters at Forbes Field, usually with a towel over his face. The conventional wisdom was that he was napping. He wasn't. One off-day, late in his career, after a thousand snickers at his presumed sloth, Clemente explained the process.

"What I like to do is lay there and think about the game we will play that night," he said. "Say Tom Seaver is going to pitch. I think about him: how he likes to pitch to me.

"I see myself at the plate. First time up, he throw me a fastball inside for a ball, then go slider away and I hit it on a line to right field for a single.

"Next time, fastball away, curve in and I see the hole between short and third and I pull the ball through it. Single. Next time, low slider . . . I hit it hard back up the middle. The fourth time, he go fastball away again, then change-up .
. . I see it coming and I wait and then I hit it down the right-field line. Double!

"In my mind, I have seen all the pitches Seaver has; I have hit against him four times. Then I get up and go out there and get four hits because I have seen all of his pitches."

A reporter listening to the explanation had asked with a grin: that's all it takes to pound Seaver, a nap?

What we never seemed to master around this place was the boo. In quainter times called the Bronx Cheer or the raspberry. Oh, you'll hear a deep grumbling on occasion and a Barry Bonds will elicit a kind of repetitious, scattered booing, but it rarely has any resonance or comes in the sort of mean, endless waves for which the fans are famous for in, say, Philadelphia.

And around here, always, the bite is removed by some amount of applause. No, hereabouts, we do not boo well. In a place where toughness is somewhat revered, perhaps booing is understood in the bones to be a bit cowardly... the booer, as it were, never required to actually challenge the booee.

We will, though, occasionally boo even our favorites... even a Clemente. And after 15 summers, the fans who had held him in abiding affection and seemingly understood him well when the press and some of his teammates didn't, booed Clemente early in the 1969 season on a day when he had struck out, hit into a pair of rally-killing doubleplays and misplayed a harmless single into a triple.

So unfamiliar was the sound to Clemente that he waved to his detractors. Equally puzzled were the denizens of the press box, one of whom said: "It took me two full minutes to realize they were booing him."

After the game, Clemente offered the booing fans a heartfelt compliment: "I'll never play for any team but this one. I could never come to Pittsburgh and play before these fans in another uniform."

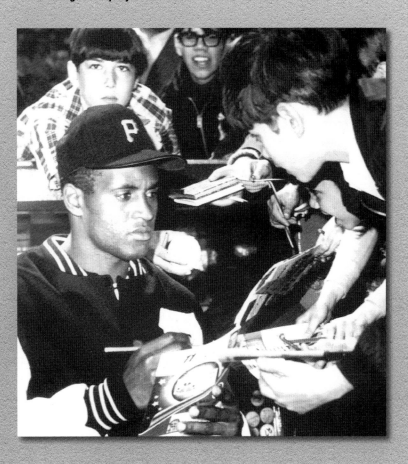

Clemente smiled wanly.

"Some nights you get four pitches you can hit and you get four hits," he said. "Some nights you get only one pitch you can hit, and I hit it because I have already seen that pitch in my mind."

Often the battering of a Seaver required more than restful visualization. One day Pirate general manager Joe L. Brown sat in the dugout and watched Clemente go through a full dress-rehearsal.

"Early one afternoon, I was at the park and Clemente was on the field by himself, standing in the batter's box," Brown related. "He'd swing the bat, drop it and run like hell for first.

"I said, 'what are you doing?' "He said, 'We're playing against Seaver tonight. I know how he will pitch me and I'm practicing what I will do and how it will be.'"

The longer he played, the more Clemente worked on visualization . . . or simply worked. Even in the 1971 season, after 16 largely splendid summers, he was still toiling to perfect the craft he honored and respected far more than most.

That July, his attorney, Elfren Bernier, was visiting from San Juan. Early one afternoon in the middle of a downpour that threatened that night's game, Clemente informed his friend they were leaving for Three Rivers Stadium immediately.

"The field will be wet tonight," he told Bernier. "I want to try a few things."

"(At the ballpark), he had someone roll the ball on the ground to make it wet and then throw it against the wall so he could practice grabbing it bare-handed," Bernier said.

"For a long time he did that. And then he ran back and forth, practicing starting and stopping."

In his baseball tour de force, Men At Work, social commentator George Will richly and repeatedly makes the point that, indeed, the game routinely requires far more effort than even the professional observer is likely to understand. As Ted Williams once inquired archly: "Don't you know how hard all this is?"

Roberto Clemente knew. And as he worked at his craft through the years leading to the fruition of that work, he was not asked about the nuances of what he was about. Rather, media concentration lingered lovingly on the easier lode to mine: his preoccupation with injuries that prevented him from full stardom. A pity, that.

Still, stardom would arrive in 1960, happily enough concurrently with the shiningest moment in a Pittsburgh sports history fairly awash in them.

Injuries slowed Clemente's ascent, particularly in 1957 when he played but 111 games and hit only .253, far below the .311 he recorded the previous season. But in the two years prior to both the Pirates and Clemente reaching the heights, he batted a solid .289 and .296.

For the man and the team, the table was set.

21

The Golden Age of Brooklyn baseball would've shone even brighter had the club not lost Roberto Clemente to the Pirates in the winter draft of 1954 The New York Giants earlier blew the opportunity to own an outfield of Clemente, Willie Mays and Henry Aaron. The Dodger error in losing Clemente was only marginally less egregious.

Ideally, Clemente would've replaced the aging Robinson and for a time, Brooklyn would've had a truly incomparable outfield. And perhaps another home-run hitter of Snider's stature. Clemente's power was to right-center field; at Ebbetts Field, the right-field fence was 297 feet from home plate.

The Dodgers of 1954—the boys of author Roger Kahn's summer— boasted two-thirds of a marvelous outfield. The previous season, Carl Furillo led the league with a .344 average and possessed the game's most feared throwing arm. Center field Duke Snider, the darling of all Flatbush, had hit .336 with 42 home runs. In left field much of the '53 season was Jackie Robinson, whose .326 average spoke only a fraction of his value to the Dodgers.

Ideally, Clemente would've replaced the aging Robinson and for a time, Brooklyn would've had a truly incomparable outfield. And perhaps another home-run hitter of Snider's stature. Clemente's power was to right-center field; at Ebbetts Field, the right-field fence was 297 feet from home plate.

As it happened, by 1957 age had overtaken Robinson, injuries sapped Furillo's production and Clemente was a Pirate.

"We had them all the way!"

Pirate broadcaster Bob Prince after each of the 21 wins the 1960 Pirates secured in the ninth inning... 12 of which came with two out.

In the reflection afforded by the passing of more than three decades, it wasn't that the Pirates brought to a baseball town that proudly traced its roots back to the turn of the century its first World championship in 35 seasons. Or since glum Calvin Coolidge sat in the Oval office.

Nor did we necessarily love them because they were an early harbinger of what was to come . . . a Golden Age that, before its flags were furled, would produce two more World Series triumphs, a pair of National League pennants, six divisional championships, four Super Bowl triumphs, a national collegiate football championship and a Heisman Trophy in a dizzying nine-year run perhaps unmatched in all the annals of sport in any town.

No, we loved them for the *how* of it. For their grit and determination to prove Yogi Berra wise beyond the laughter that ensued when he insisted, so thoughtfully, that "it ain't over till it's over." And for their swagger: Outfielder Gino Cimoli walking into hotel lobbies on the road in mid-summer shouting, "The big, bad Buccos are in town!"

Rarely if ever has baseball had a livelier would-be corpse than the 1960 Pittsburgh Pirates. Decapitated, they would not die—21 of their 95 victories coming in the ninth. So that you came to believe they would somehow find a way to win, and were genuinely surprised when they didn't. So that as they kept reversing the course in the gloaming of game after game, you took to not tuning Bob Prince in until the late innings. One mid-year doubleheader defined them as a club. Trailing Cincinnati, 5-0, with two outs in the ninth, they ran off six quick runs to take the nightcap. In the first game, they had erased a Cincinnati lead in the 10th to win.

Indeed they were—as the peerless Red Smith wrote in early October when it must've become apparent to the New York Yankees that they were messing with something being decided on a higher plane—"destiny's darlings."

The Forbes Field chant was "charge" and the war cry was "Beat 'em, Bucs!" And across a glorious summer—by measurement, it rained far less in 1960 than usual—the Bucs did both. Arguably that fine summer Roberto Clemente was, in the vernacular, the team's glue. Not in the sense that he provided it with its style, which was raucous and so bold that, at a team party, third baseman Don Hoak loudly suggested to a beautiful redhead in front a large audience, which incidentally included her husband, that they publicly consummate their five-minute relationship. Nor was Clemente a leader in a clubhouse presided over by the fiery Hoak and a core of young veterans that included Bill Mazeroski, Dick Groat, Bob Skinner, Bill Virdon and others. But when the 1960 Pirates began to founder, as often as not it was Clemente that righted the ship.

Two months into the season, he was hitting .353 and leading the National League. A few weeks later, he crashed into a concrete abutment making a catch that preserved a shutout for Vinegar Bend Mizell and had to be hospitalized. A seven-game lead over Milwaukee all but evaporated; Clemente returned to the lineup five days later and within a week, the Pirates again led by seven. When they lost four in a row just before a West Coast trip later in the summer, he hit home runs in three successive games and the Pirates swaggered anew.

On September 25th in Milwaukee—where the year before they had fallen apart and yielded their pennant hopes—the Pirates clinched their first National League pennant since Coolidge was in office. Clemente ignored a stop sign at third base a minute or so after a St. Louis loss had assured the Pirates the title.

"I want to get on the bench and talk about the pennant," he explained.

In Pittsburgh...pandemonium. A drunk commandeered a streetcar and wheeled it about the city for two hours before submitting to arrest with a huge smile. A hundred-thousand fans met the Pirate flight returning from Milwaukee. But the serious celebration awaited. The Yankees were coming...and all of Pittsburgh was waiting for them.

To understand what the 1960 Pirates meant to Pittsburgh, it is necessary to know something of the 20th century history of the place and a bit about its psyche. In the truest sense, it is not the "melting pot" so many politicians have suggested, but rather the richest of ethnic stews. An admixture with little loss of identity. The city's more than 80 neighborhoods mostly retained their ethnic distinctiveness. Bloomfield was Italian, Mt. Washington German, Lawrenceville Slavic, Garfield Irish and so forth.

Since the advent of steel—even in 1960, more than half of the *world's* steel was made within a 75-mile radius of the city—Pittsburgh had been known as the Smoky City. But "smoky" was simply a euphemism for dirty. Steel was made there because of the rich lode of iron and other metals beneath its hills, and because the Allegheny and Monongahela rivers framing the city provided cheap transportation to major markets.

Steel making was a hot and grimy business. For mile after mile along the rivers, mills going around the clock belched smoke and flame a hundred-feet high into the night skies and in many places at midnight, you could read a newspaper on the sidewalk without benefit of artificial light.

It was not uncommon for four generations of men in a single family to have worked nowhere but a steel mill. Sons routinely followed fathers and grandfathers to the open hearths and in time it became a rough-hewn place of thick forearms and bone-deep pride in who and what you were.

The work was desperately hard, the pleasures raucously simple. Even the food and drink reflected the innate toughness of the place. Kielbasa, a spicy smoked sausage guaranteed to induce heartburn in the less robust, and Iron City, a local beer vigorous enough to cut the grime in a man's mouth after a 4-to-midnight shift, were easily the most popular comestibles. Even clothing was largely basic...thick wool surpassing worsted; cotton favored and silk seen as pretentious. The iron imperative of the place was hard work and getting things done. Talking the talk without fully demonstrating an ability to walk the walk was widely held to be unseemly. Honor, then, was not an uncommon trait.

Still, the dirt and smoke pouring from the mills was inescapable, so that by afternoon it could be shaken from sheer curtains hung clean that morning.

Wrote famed British author Anthony Trollope after visiting just before the turn of the 20th century: "I was never more in love with dirt and smoke than when I stood here and watched the darkness of night close in upon the floating soot which hovered over the housetops of the city."

A kind of collective inferiority complex grew from that. To the rest of the world, Pittsburgh exported steel and machine politicians and was otherwise known, not for the grit and resiliency and bedrock loyalty of its people, but for uncleanliness.

Pittsburgh was simply out there on the backside of the Alleghenies where the ferrous metals had reached up close to the earth's crust, but still short of the country's meaningful heartland. An undistinguished place, really. Like some sort of

In the decades since Mazeroski's historic home run, it has been argued that indeed, New York columnist Red Smith had been right in observing that destiny had taken a hand in the 1960 World Series in behalf of the Pirates.

As Pirate outfielder and club bon vivant Gino Cimoli put it, "they set all the records, but we won the games, baby." The Yankees had won their three games by a combined 35 runs; the Pirates had won their four by seven. Fate alone? To a person, the more than 1 million celebrants who came into the Golden Triangle area of Downtown following the seventh game heartily disagreed. Those currently living still do.

So did a forgotten bartender in Torreon, Mexico. That evening, a house painter named Antonio Duenas walked into a Torreon bar and said glumly, "the Yankees gave it away!"

The bartender—a Pirate fan—shot him dead.

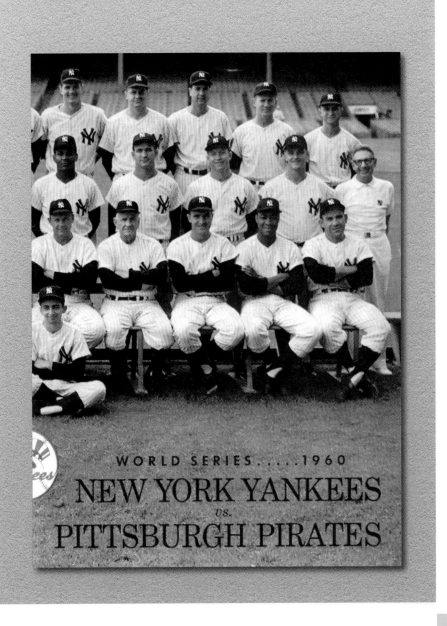

WORLD SERIES.....1960
NEW YORK YANKEES
vs.
PITTSBURGH PIRATES

daft family member, to be acknowledged when absolutely necessary, but surely not to be paraded about. As a character sniffed in a movie of the day, "Nobody is from *Pittsburgh*, Serena!"

So it was that in 1960, this city was ready to clasp a baseball team to its busom in an embrace very few others have ever mustered; to celebrate it... ready for its accomplishments to bolster public esteem, for it to get things done. And, in the case of the Yankees, maybe to get some vengeance. Local folk legend held that 33 years before in their last World Series appearance, the Pirates had watched Ruth and Gehrig and Lazzeri and Irish Bob Meusel take batting practice before the first game and folded their tents, losing four straight.

If he understandably failed to fully appreciate what was at stake for Pittsburgh in 1960, it certainly didn't impede Roberto Clemente's performance. He got nine hits and hit safely in all seven games of what actually was an Autumnal classic. And one full of the sort of irony the locals loved. New York won three laughers—16-3, 10-0 and 12-0; the Pirates won four nail biters, the last one in fitting fashion for a club which could prevail with a stake in its heart.

When the Pirates erased the second of two Yankee leads, Clemete's infield single scored a run and kept alive the rally that gave the Pirates a lead and set the stage for Mazeroski, still some 34 years later the best-loved athlete in a place almost overrun with them.

In the bottom of the ninth, the quiet, private second baseman with arguably the game's most sure glove hit a Ralph Terry fastball slightly more than 406 feet into some maple trees that framed the picturesque left field wall at Forbes Field.

Later it was called "the shot heard 'round the world" and if that is a bit melodramatic for even the most dramatic home run in baseball history, it continues to reverberate in a city that needed something like it.

Pittsburgh, of course, erupted. In three hours, not a drop of liquor was left in any Downtown bar. It was estimated that more than one million people—or almost twice the city's actual population—poured into the center city before officials sealed it off. They came, it was written in the newspapers, like a tide. Caught up in boisterous celebration, the mayor swung an elbow wildly and knocked his wife momentarily unconscious. Later, when they heard Mickey Mantle had wept all the way back to New York on the Yankee plane, they rejoiced even more.

And Roberto Clemente, relatively new to the setting and surely unaware of its deepest meanings, did a curious and meaningful thing.

Amidst the abandon of the Pirate clubhouse, he quickly dressed and left to join the throngs.

"I feel like one of them," he said of the Pirate fans, whose revelry was almost indescribable. "I never see anything like them."

When there was some criticism of Clemente's early departure from the ranks of the Pirate celebrants, he didn't understand it.

"I want to be with the people who pay my salary," he said. "I shake hands with my players and everything, show them how happy I was. But I have no words to say how I feel when I went outside with the fans."

In that sweet season, Roberto Clemente hit .314 and drove in 94 runs. And he stood just in the suburbs of what writer Leonard Gardner called Fat City.

21

Early in his major-league career, Roberto Clemente came under the not-so-tender ministrations of manager Bobby Bragan, an eccentric man. The Pirates of that era were a woebegone assortment of wannabes and never-weres, Clemente the only real hope for the future.

Bragan's zeal to win finally did him in before Clemente's future could be realized. In 1957, the Pirates could hit but couldn't pitch or play much defense and, as Bragam simmered, threatened to become the 10th Pirate team in 12 seasons to finish either last or next-to-last. With four .300 hitters in the lineup, the Pirates fell into last place in June and Bragan boiled over.

One night in Cincinnati, suspecting Reds' pitcher Raul Sanchez of throwing a spit-ball, Bragan dispatched two Pirates to the mound with a bucket of water. For the fourth time that season, he was ejected. A few weeks later, thrown out of yet another game, Bragan returned and offered a soft drink to the plate umpire. Four days later, he was fired.

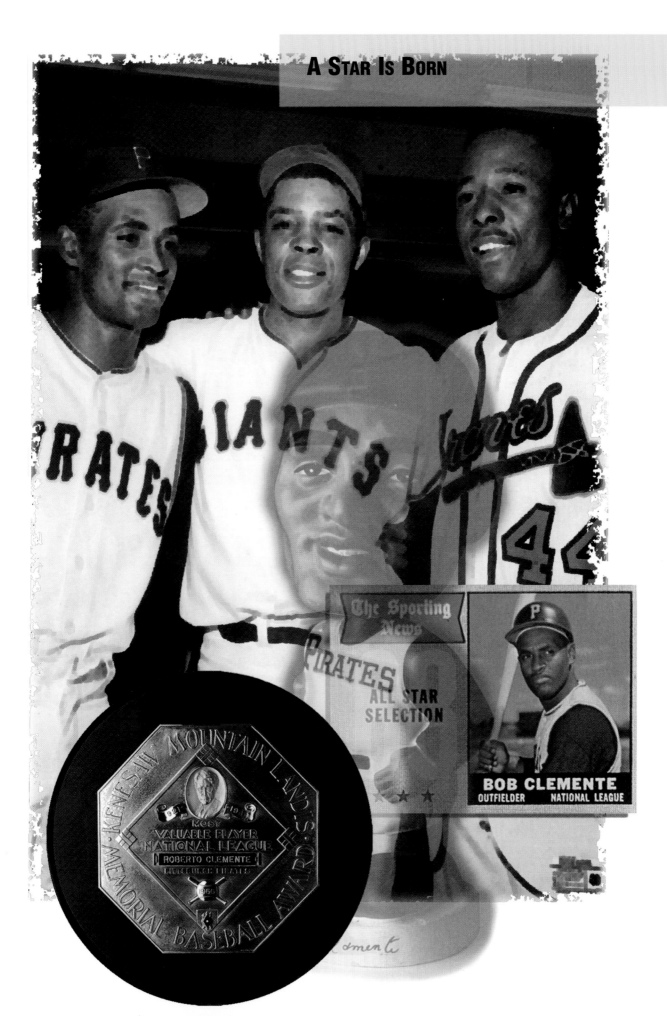

The Sporting News
PIRATES
ALL STAR
SELECTION

BOB CLEMENTE
OUTFIELDER   NATIONAL LEAGUE

Greatness in any field of endeavor does not have its arrival heralded at a particular moment. Nobody tears a page from a calendar and proclaims that on this or that day or week or month so-and-so has crossed the threshold and thereafter should carry the label of greatness. No, greatness, as opposed to mere competence, crosses the pale by that plodding conveyance, time, and creeps into public awareness only with the slow passage of the years. One day it is simply acknowledged, as though it had been there all the while. A body of those with unassailable credentials to render such judgments speaks out.

In baseball, a Rusty Staub talks to a respected New York sportswriter; a story appears and later is widely disseminated by a wire service. Heads start to nod; comparisons begin to be made. Greatness is finally conferred by silent consensus. The label becomes largely indelible.

So it was with Roberto Clemente. In 1960, he had been a big cog in the Pirate machinery, but one of a number of gears, nevertheless. In 1961, he became the fuel.

In the All-Star game that summer, he tripled, drove in a run with a 400-foot sacrifice, and singled in the game-winning run. That season he hit .351 to claim the first of his four batting titles and authored 23 home runs, then a career high.

As the 1960 World Champions began to fall apart, Clemente pushed toward acknowledged greatness. He had 200 hits for the first time, 63 for extra bases, and drove in 89 runs while missing only nine games. In 1964, following two more banner seasons, a .339 average brought the second batting championship. The Gold Gloves began to accumulate in the family game room. Of the great outfielders who came into the game following World War 2—Mays, Aaron, Mantle, Carl Yastrzemski, Frank Robinson—none was Clemente's superior and perhaps only Mays his equal as the complete player.

Still, for every orchestra there is the ideal conductor, and until Danny Murtaugh retired because of poor health in 1965, Clemente had gone without his.

For the symphony that was Roberto Clemente, the ideal man to wave the baton was Harry Walker. Nicknamed The Hat. One of the finest slap hitters of his time. And a man who keenly appreciated Clemente's yearning to be separated from the pack of merely good players. For decades, Harry Walker had been known publicly and around baseball merely as "Dixie Walker's brother." He knew an identity crisis when he saw one.

Harry Walker could've sold refrigerators to Eskimos. Alabama-born and raised, honeysuckle dripped from the endless torrent of words that poured from his mouth. That in time he became a sportscaster surprised not a single soul. Job was no better suited to suffering locusts.

From the moment of his arrival in Pittsburgh in 1965 to replace Murtaugh, Walker was effusive in his praise of Clemente.

"He always busts his butt," Harry Walker would say, and to a player there is no greater praise.

For years, Murtaugh and Clemente had been antagonists, perhaps understandably enough. Murtaugh was a tough Irisher from the mills of hardscrabble Chester County in Southeastern Pennsylvania. The bread lines of the Depression remained vivid in his memory. As a player, he had spit tobacco juice on his wounds and continued to play a gritty if undistinguished second base. He adhered strictly to the baseball tenet of his day: You did not talk about injuries, you ignored them.

From another culture, Clemente took at face-value the inquiry "How are you?" Asked, he was pleased to tell, often at some length. To Murtaugh, preoccupation with matters of health was untoward, even unmanly; to Clemente, they were both interesting and deeply personal. On his wounds, Roberto Clemente spat not tobacco juice but rhetoric. The rift between the two very different men never healed until Murtaugh returned to manage the Pirates a third time in 1970.

But in Harry Walker there was something of a psychologist. Where Murtaugh didn't, he sensed that

Clemente had run afoul of the baseball tradition that, in theory anyway, argues that players must be treated equally. It wasn't that Clemente sought special treatment; it was that he demanded to be treated as an individual.

What to Murtaugh was heresy was to Walker accommodation. Under Murtaugh, the fiat was that all outfielders took part in pre-game fielding drills, something Clemente needed the way ducks require swimming practice. Walker was subtle: "Robby, go out and shag for a while. You don't need the work but the other guys do and if you're not out there, they'll loaf."

Publicly, Walker told reporters: "I wish I had a dozen like him. He's high-spirited, a thoroughbred. He needs to be treated differently. But things mean a lot more to him than people ever realized."

When Clemente insisted the Forbes Field batter's box was at fault for a brief slump—a complaint which would've enraged Murtaugh—Walker had the sand base replaced with clay and just smiled when Clemente hit .444 over the next month.

The easiest of riders, Walker prodded gently: Clemente responded. In two seasons, baseball people—if not quite yet the fans—began to realize Clemente was separating himself from the pack. The game's insiders acknowledged that he was, by the end of the 1966 season, arguably the finest all-around player in the game.

"Some people Harry didn't reach," said Pirate GM Joe Brown, "but Roberto he did. He convinced Roberto he could become one of the great players of all time."

Clemente convinced everyone else. In the voting for the 1966 most valuable player award in the National League, Dodger pitcher Sandy Koufax was favored. He had won 27 games with an arthritic left arm, had a microscopic 1.74 earned-run-average and completed no fewer than 27 games. Still, Clemente edged him in the voting despite playing for a third-place club. No one else was within hailing distance, including three of the very finest players of the post-war era—Mays, Henry Aaron and young Pete Rose.

In accepting the MVP award, Roberto Clemente remained true to his own code. Bitterly disappointed not at having failed to win it in the championship season of 1960 but at finishing ninth in the balloting, he never wore his '60 Series ring. He was typically outspoken.

"It is the highest honor a player can hope for," he said, "but I was expecting it. Sure I am bitter about about 1960. I carried the club the whole year. (But) if I had not won the MVP, I would not have been mad because Sandy Koufax was a great pitcher and he deserved it.

"And I tell you one thing, I didn't win the MVP alone. I was sad because we didn't win the pennant (the Pirates finished third with a 92-70 record) but I thought the MVP was something the whole ballclub could be proud of because it gave our whole team recognition."

Harry Walker, who despite Clemente's protest would be fired the following year, understood that response.

"He won the MVP because he did so many little things," Walker said. "He did the things so many stars don't . . . hustling on routine ground balls, breaking up double plays, taking the extra base. He has pride . . . he wants people to know what he's accomplished."

Rusty Staub knew. Within the game, everyone knew: Roberto Clemente had become baseball's Main Man. Ironically enough, five years later and after 16 largely brilliant summers, he would become an overnight sensation.

Once, after covering him for years, a writer wrote of Clemente: "He always reminded me of an African prince, standing in the surf and brandishing a spear at a retreating slave ship."

He was not the only one to see a majestic side; in eulogizing Clemente, then commissioner Bowie Kuhn made reference to it, as did others across the years.

Certainly he had the look of royalty. Skin the color of burnished mahogany, high cheekbones, eyes that flashed whatever emotion roiled him at the moment. An almost palpable pride carried as a gonfalon. The body of a light-heavyweight in perfect proportion, just under 5-11, just over 175 pounds. Broad, sloping shoulders; an expansive, chiseled chest; the tapered waist of a ballerina flowing into quarter-miler's legs.

"What God had in mind there," teammate Steve Blass once said, "was a ballplayer."

Odd, then, that He should've incorporated into that ballplayer the sort of sensitivity that often produces poets. Few knew it, but for hours at a time, Clemente would roam the beaches of Puerto Rico in the off-season searching for oddly-shaped pieces of driftwood.

"Why do you waste your time with that... it is just wood?" a friend once inquired.

"You are crazy!" Clemente shouted. "Yes it is wood. But you don't see what I see. You don't feel about it what I feel. You can take it and shape it, and it is you."

And the man who would sand and polish driftwood also made ceramic figurines and played a fair organ and collected delicately crafted bottles from as far away as Italy. As Vera Clemente said of her husband, "When he plays baseball, he does it from the heart; he does everything that way."

Approaching the 1971 season, his fire for the game had not been banked. If recurring back and elbow injuries had all but ruined the 1968 season—Clemente hit a mere .291—he fairly shredded National League pitching throughout the 1960s. And he aged like prime wine. In 1967 he was hitting .390 near the all-star break and then posted a .385 average the final month to win his third batting title. Had the Pirates played nothing but afternoon games, he probably would've hit more than .400. In 68 daylight games, he hit .411.

In 1969 (.345 and 91 RBI) and 1970 (.352), he nearly won batting titles, his style as undisciplined as ever. Pete Rose barely beat out a bunt in his final at-bat of the '69 season to deny Clemente the batting crown.

"Roberto can hit any pitch, anywhere, at any time," Sandy Koufax said. "He will hit pitchouts. He will hit brushback pitches. He will hit high, inside pitches to the opposite field… which would be ridiculous even if he didn't do it with both feet off the ground."

Those summers between the 1966 MVP award and the 1971 campaign signaled the coming Golden Age of sports in Pittsburgh. Clemente's fielding and throwing improved with age. Mays' skills had sadly eroded; Aaron's never were a match for Clemente's; ruined knees had driven Mantle from the game. The best defensive outfielder in baseball was, remarkably enough, in the twilight of his 30s. As Houston's Bob Watson had said, "It's not so bad being robbed by Jesse James."

As was noted in the prologue, far too much attention was paid to Clemente's injuries by the news media, the fans and some of his teammates.

Although he talked about those injuries at some length, it must also be noted that: He played more games than any other Pirate, that across 18 seasons he averaged 135 games a year during a career in which the 154-game season was the rule for almost half his career,and that the person best-positioned to make such judgments, longtime Pirate trainer Tony Bartirome, dismisses suggestions that Clemente, in the vernacular of the game, "jaked it."

Before he retired, Bartirome addressed the notion that Clemente suffered from hypochondria:

"How the hell could he have been a hypochondriac? He played with injuries other guys wouldn't have come to the ballpark with, because he knew his presence made a difference.

"I've seen him play with Achilles tendons stretched tighter than a drum. One year he had a bad knee, all swollen and stiff. I told him not to play; that he could be out for weeks if he did, or jeopardize his career. 'No,' he said, 'we need a few wins.'

"He got hurt by the drive he put into the game . . . any game. He played every game the same, hard. He played a whole season down there (Puerto Rico) every year and for him, there wasn't any difference between the winter league and the big league.

"Hell, he played twice as many games as Aaron or Mays.

"Once I burned him with a hydroculator pad... left an awful-looking scar. He didn't even make a fuss.

"Hypochondriac ... shit."

Even the lack of national recognition, for so long an irritant to his considerable pride, had with the passing of time become mostly an insoluble riddle.

"I play as good as anybody… .but I am not loved," Clemente said one night in 1970, although he surely was in Pittsburgh, if not beyond it. "I don't need to be loved. I wish it would happen. Do you know what I mean?"

Sadly, his meaning was clear. He had said and done things that resulted in a stranger being projected to the public rather than the man he saw himself to be.

"I need recognition," he admitted. "I need people to respect me."

By the Autumn of 1971, unquestionably they would. That summer, he was Merlin, bringer of magic to the ballpark. Or Pan, flinging himself about effortlessly. And the respected elder statesman of a club that had suddenly come of age as a pennant contender and which had coalesced around him.

For the first time, perhaps, Roberto Clemente was as important off the field as he was on it.

When young power-hitting Bob Robertson tailed off dramatically after a superb season the previous year, Clemente applied the lash:

"You quit on us! You had a big year, then you strut around. You should take batting practice at two o'clock… go out again at four… hit with the extra men at six! Sit on the bench and study the pitchers.

Clemente jogs, Baltimore pitcher Mike Cuellar fumes.

"When you get here, you don't stop doing the things you did that got you here. Listen, the first year, they don't think about you. Then, you get established and they start thinking about you, and talking about you."

When the relief pitching threatened at mid-year to unravel what Willie Stargell's record-setting home run pace and Dock Ellis' nearly-unhittable pitching had woven, Clemente again took a hand.

"The club needed Mudcat Grant that year and he was struggling," said Nellie King, the Pirate radio and television analyst. "One night he gave up a grand slam to Bill Buckner and cost us a game. Clemente had four or five hits that night. Anyway, I'm still in the clubhouse after almost everybody had left and Roberto got a stool and went over and sat beside Mudcat.

"He kept telling him, 'You can pitch! You can still get people out! Forget this game, it is gone.'"

Later, Grant, who returned to form and became the principal set-up man in the bullpen, said: "He held my hand emotionally when I needed it. It was the warmest thing anyone ever did for me in baseball."

But when the Pirates again faltered that summer, Clemente took the tack he had with Robertson.

"He would start saying, 'Hey, we're not doing this... hey we're not doing that,'" relief pitcher Dave Giusti said. "Other guys tried to do that. But, hell, who were you going to listen to?"

A slew of young hitters—Richie Hebner, Dave Cash, Al Oliver and Robertson—had productive seasons. Stargell barely cooled from a pace which produced 30 home runs by the all-star break and finished with 48 and 125 RBI. Rennie Stennett came up at mid-season and hit .353 in the last 50 games. The Pirate reserves were such that Sport magazine ran a cover story on them called "Thunder From The Bench." Roberto Clemente drove in 86 runs and, and at the doddering baseball age of 37, batted a remarkable .341.

And he had just gotten started.

As they had in the 1960 classic, the Pirates stumbled leaving the World Series gate, losing the first two games to Baltimore, even though Clemente had four hits in nine at-bats. But as they had in 1960, the Pirates recovered nicely.

They won game three, 5-1, when Clemente legged out a leadoff tap back to the mound in the pivotal inning, his hustle triggering a wild throw to first base. Moments later, Robertson misread a bunt sign and hit the ball out of the park to sink the Orioles.

In the next two games, Clemente had key hits in Pirate wins, as well as saving one game with a sliding catch along the right field foul line and a preserving the second with a throw to third base that Oriole Davey Johnson called "the greatest throw I ever saw."

In the seventh game, Clemente hit his second home run of the Series to give the Pirates a lead and they never trailed, Steve Blass pitching a superb four-hitter. And, in the nation's newspapers and on its television sets, after 17 sparkling summers, Roberto Clemente became, as they say, an overnight sensation.

His 1971 World Series summary looked like this: a .414 batting average; two truly remarkable catches; one throw for posterity; two home runs and a third mistakenly called a foul ball by umpire John Kibler; the automobile given to the Series MVP; and, most important of all, the widespread public recognition previously withheld. His post-game comments had a singular theme.

"I want everyone in the world to know that this is the way I play all of the time," he said. And said. And said some more, lest the sporting press fail to comprehend the message.

"All season, every season, I gave everything I had to this game. The press call me a crybaby, hypochondriac… they say I'm not a team player.

"Now everyone knows the way Roberto Clemente plays."

But few knew how he thought. Nellie King got a glimpse of the process the night before the World Series began when he and his wife rode in an elevator with Clemente and Willie Stargell.

"He was telling Willie, 'You can relax, if you cannot hit, I will carry the team,'" King recalled. "I told my wife that night, 'He's getting Willie relaxed so he won't have to carry the team.' It wasn't bragging. He knew he could do it."

For Clemente, Blass, Manny Sanguillen and Pittsburgh…Jubilation.

On the Pirate charter back from Baltimore, Clemente embraced Blass, who in just a matter of months would movingly eulogize him in a Puerto Rican church.

"It was a very personal moment for me," Blass said. "So many miles… so many ballgames. I didn't know what to say. I just held on."

As Roberto Clemente had. Held on until the distance closed between what he saw in himself and what others came to see. Held on until his performance scraped off the unwarranted labels of malingerer and malcontent. Held on until, after all those seasons, recognition for what he was and what he had been finally came along.

And held on until his contemporaries had all long since retired. Everyone fully understood when the game's Boswell, Roger Angell, wrote that Roberto Clemente played "a kind of baseball that none of us had ever seen before."

21

On the 50th anniversary of Roberto Clemente's birth—August 18, 1984—the United States Postal Service issued a postage stamp in his memory.

More than 80,000 stamps were sold in Carolina, Puerto Rico—Clemente's birthplace—on the first day they became available to the public. Another half-million were sold in Pittsburgh. They remain popular among baseball memorabilia collectors.

Roberto is now one of the players in major league history to get 3000 or more hits

Baseball has been played professionally—that is to say for money—for more than 110 years. Or since the time when players on the road slept two to a bed. The day the Sioux overran Custer at the Little Bighorn, Chicago was playing at Cincinnati. Over the years, roughly 13,000 players have reached the major leagues. Nineteen of them have managed to accumulate 3000 hits. Roberto Clemente was the 11th.

Before him: Ty Cobb, Stan Musial, Tris Speaker, Honus Wagner, Henry Aaron, Eddie Collins, Nap Lajoie, Willie Mays, Paul Waner, Cap Anson. After him: Pete Rose, Carl Yastrzemski, Al Kaline, George Brett, Lou Brock, Rod Carew, Robin Yount, Dave Winfield.

To give you an idea of the scope of that accomplishment, missing just a few games each summer, a player could hit .295 every season for 20 straight years and not manage it. He could have 200 hits per season—and in some win a batting championship—for 14 consecutive years and not even come close to the 3000 plateau. As Ted Williams inquired, "Don't you know how hard this all is?"

Few if any athletic accomplishments exceed the 3000-hit milestone. Mere overriding ability will not do it. Dozens of Hall of Fame players failed to reach it. Ruth. Gehrig. DiMaggio. Obviously something far greater than simple longevity is required. Certainly sheer persistence is a requisite. That, Roberto Clemente had.

If in the previous year he had solidified his position in the game, then in 1972 he sought lasting achievement, a place in baseball's Valhalla.

Hit No. 3000

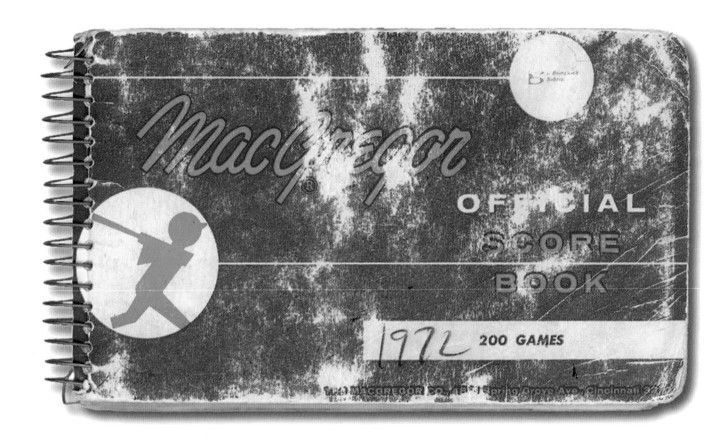

Pirate beat writer Bob Smizik's scorebook from an historic day. Late in the game, Bill Mazeroski pinch-hit for a weary Clemente.

It took considerable doing. In June, he was diagnosed as suffering from a rheumatoid condition in both heels. In July, he got the flu and later a stomach virus. In August, he strained both Achilles' tendons. One day, Pirate official Joe O'Toole removed a wax figure of Clemente from a Three Rivers Stadium display and placed it on the trainer's table before a night game. Even Clemente had to laugh.

Still, he missed 47 of the Pirates' first 116 games and there was talk of his retirement. He said what all players do at that stage in a lengthy career: "I'll play as long as I can help the ballclub."

Although the Pirates were in a race for their third consecutive National League East championship, Clemente went into the final 26 games needing 25 hits to reach the 3000 mark.

Fittingly, he got No. 2999 against future Hall of Famer Steve Carlton in Philadelphia in the Pirates' final road game of the season and was immediately replaced so the historic hit could come in Pittsburgh.

Ironically enough, No. 3000 was delayed by the late Luke Quay's single brush with baseball lore. The soft-spoken and witty Quay was the sports editor of the McKeesport Daily News, a small paper in a mill valley town, and had been covering the Pirates for a decade. A writer who rarely sought out the sensational, he had formed a bond with a number of Pirates and became a Clemente confidante. Quay had arranged to be the official scorer for the home games following the Pirate trip to Philadelphia in order to participate in a piece of baseball history.

In a Sept. 29th at-bat that might've produced hit no. 3000, Clemente pushed a roller to New York Met second baseman Ken Boswell, who bobbled it. The Three Rivers crowd to a customer stared at the scoreboard. In the press box, Quay's call was immediate: "E-4… error, Boswell." Inexplicably, the "H" sign flickered on the scoreboard and disappeared. The crowd erupted, rolls of toilet paper streaming from the upper decks, waves of applause rising, falling, and rising again, like waves crashing endlessly against a pier.

Then, history, too, suffered a jolt. Quay's ruling appeared on the scoreboard... error, second baseman. At that juncture, local legend shoved its way to the stage.

Pittsburgh baseball lore of the day held that former Pirate great Paul Waner, in a bid for his 3000th hit, had been awarded it on a scratch infield single and had supposedly waved toward the press box to signal that he did not want such an occasion marred by a chintzy product. The official scorer that day is said to have reversed his decision, and later Waner got the historical hit with a more robust effort.

In the clubhouse afterwards, still without his piece of history, and after some griping, Clemente admitted he held a similar perspective.

"I want it to be a clean basehit," he told Quay privately. "If I had known who was scoring, I wouldn't have complained. I really didn't want the hit like that, anyway."

The next afternoon, the situation became moot. Against young Met left-hander Jon Matlack, who had not allowed Clemente a hit in 1972, he rammed a curve ball stiff to the gap in left-center for the hit that put him in the pantheon.

The amenities were observed, the ball stored in first base coach Don Leppert's left hip pocket for posterity, and Clemente dedicated the hit to "the fans of Pittsburgh and Puerto Rico and the man who made me play baseball, Roberto Marin."

The scoreboard reflected the rare accomplishment. Stark numbers simply read: 3000.

Sadly enough, there would be no 3001.

Roberto is now one of 11 players in major league history to get 3000 or more hits

Reaching the 3000-hit mark qualifies a major-league hitter for baseball's pantheon, but getting 2000 hits is hardly small change. In 1966, when Roberto Clemente got his 2000th, only 115 others in baseball history had managed that accomplishment.

Hit No. 1000 had come in 1961 off Cincinnati pitcher Ken Hunt. In the Reds' bullpen, pitcher and later celebrated baseball author Jim Brosnan took note.

"That's Clemente's 1000," he remarked to teammate Bill Henry.

"Did he get 'em all off us?" inquired the laconic Texan.

Clemente's 2000th came at the expense of Chicago Hall of Famer Ferguson Jenkins, a three-run homer to win a game in Pittsburgh in September amidst a two-team pennant race with Los Angeles.

If the Pirates lost that race in the final two weeks of the season, Clemente took a certain satisfaction from the fact that, in his first decade, he hit .375 against the Dodgers.

Ironically enough, Clemente's first major-league hit came at the Dodgers' expense: an infield single in the hole at short off Brooklyn lefthander Johnny Podres, currently the Los Angeles pitching coach.

Death is mostly an ordinary business. Disease or injury occur, body parts wear too badly to function, dying follows either slowly or quickly. Relatively few pause to notice; the world moves smartly along. Occasionally, fate seems to take a hand in a macabre fashion, death occurring only if a chain of events remains unbroken. It happened that way to Roberto Clemente, whose passing triggered a covey of "ifs."

The facts of his death are without dispute: He was one of five men who perished about 9:30 p.m. Atlantic Standard Time on the evening of Dec. 31, 1972 when an old airplane full of eight tons of relief supplies for the survivors of a Nicaraguan earthquake crashed into the sea about a mile from the San Juan International Airport.

In reflection, it seems reasonable, perhaps even certain, that if even one in a series of occurrences had been different, death would have come to him at another time.

Ifs. More than two decades after Clemente's death, they continue to linger:

If the DC-7 had been test flown after having two propellers replaced, the accident almost surely would not have happened…

Melchor Clemente at memorial service

If the regular pilot, Bill Shearer, had not gone home to Charleston, South Carolina for the holidays…

If two of the three-man crew—owner and co-pilot Art Rivera and flight engineer Frank Matias—had been certified for their duties…

If Nicaraguan dictator Anastasio Somoza had not called the Clemente home at 5 a.m., asking him to make the trip…

If pilot Dave Joyner had not just bought a new $200 suit for a party that night and had not turned down Rivera's plea to fly as the co-pilot…

If Clemente had not continued to wonder over the fate of a legless Nicaraguan boy for whom he'd arranged to receive artificial limbs…

If the premonitions of Roberto Jr. and his grandfather, Melchor Clemente, had been respected…

And, in retrospect, even if airport tower officials had listened to Air Indies pilot Tom Klocinski…

Had any single factor in that list of "ifs" been different, Roberto Clemente probably would not have died on a mission of mercy.

But they were not.

The DC-7 sporting new props was not flight-tested, even after a 16-hour delay in takeoff was caused by first faulty lights and then fouled spark plugs on the number 3 engine.

Meanwhile, there were reportedly 6000 dead in Managua and many more thousands injured. Relief supplies gathered by Clemente and shipped by boat to Nicaragua were rumored being sold from the docks by Somoza's soldiers.

By telephone that morning, Somoza had told Clemente his country would only accept money and food. "That made Roberto think the military was getting supplies shipped from Puerto Rico," Clemente's attorney said. "He was enraged. He said, 'I'll go down there and distribute the supplies myself!'"

Shearer didn't return from South Carolina and Joyner had a party to attend.

"Shearer was adamant that plane be test-flown," said Joyner, then a pilot for Shamrock Air Freight in San Juan. "If Bill had been there, Art would've unloaded that plane and Bill would've tested it. (But) Art was desperate for a crew. I had just spent $200 on a suit and we'd been planning to go to this party. I turned him down."

There were other "ifs." In Managua the previous winter, Clemente had managed a Puerto Rican team in the World Amateur Baseball Championships and had been royally treated. And while there he had visited a hospital and formed a bond with a legless little boy.

Above, right: Wife Vera and mother Luisa with Clemente sons: Roberto, Jr., Enrique and Luis. Above: Puerto Rican people mourn.

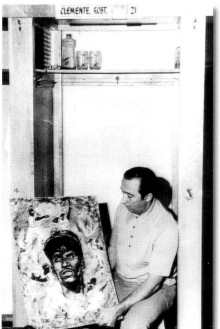

Above: Luisa and Vera Clemente at Three Rivers Stadium tribute. Left: Trainer Tony Bartirome with Clemente portrait

"He would say to Vera, 'I wonder how the kid is… I wonder how the kid is,'" recalled Luis Mayoral.

As preparations for the flight were being made, one of Clemente's sons and 92-year old Melchor Clemente had dreams about it.

"Daddy's going to Nicaragua but he's not coming back," seven-year-old Roberto Jr. told his grandmother after awakening from a nap. "Don't let him go."

Only weeks from his own death, Clemente's father told his wife, "I had a dream the airplane crashed into the sea."

That New Year's Eve, several Pirates were attending a party in pitcher Bob Johnson's 27th floor apartment overlooking the Atlantic near the airport. They idly watched flares falling just off Isla Verde, a five-mile ribbon of land that runs from the airport to the tourist hotels of nearby Condado.

"We saw search crews looking for debris and bodies," said Pirate outfielder Richie Zisk. "We talked about what a terrible New Year's Eve for the people who knew the victims."

And for Klocinski, the Air Indies pilot whose plane had left the San Juan airport directly behind Rivera's DC-7. It is generally conceded that co-pilot Art Rivera had made a fatal error in retracting the flaps rather than the landing gear after two engines on the DC-7 exploded just after takeoff, but Klocinski argued for years that another error, equally lethal, might have been made.

Returning to San Juan after his nightly 45-minute flight to Mayaguez, Klocinski argued that the Coast Guard had searched for the DC-7 miles from where he had seen it crash and float in the waters off Pinonas Beach near Point Maldonado.

"Hell, they were five miles away," Klocinski said. "I had circled the plane in the water and asked if they wanted me to stay, but they (tower officials) said the Coast Guard knew where the plane was and was on its way. "Three times in four hours after I got back, I asked if I could be of assistance. They told me to forget it. It's my opinion there was no one alive after impact, but if anyone had been unconscious in the tail section... that would've been another matter."

Interviewed two years after the accident, Klocinski— who earlier had spent four years with a civilian airline in Southeast Asia and had flown dozens of search-and-rescue missions—remained bitter about the experience.

"The day after the accident," he said, "I was called and asked if I would help locate where the plane went down. I showed them."

Few traces were found: pilot Jerry Hill's body; sections of the cockpit and fuselage; Hill's glasses; a sock belonging to Clemente; and, a week later, his brief-case. Killed were: Roberto Clemente, honorary chairman of the Nicaraguan Relief Committee in Puerto Rico; a friend, San Juan trucking executive Rafael Lozano; and the crew of three, Hill, Rivera and Matias.

Top, left: U.S. Navy divers take a break in search for wreakage. Top, right: Memorial wreath left at crash site by children. Right: Pirate office staff sorts mail from grieving fans. Above: Diver locates section of DC-7 on ocean floor.

A hearing some years later found no one culpable.

Eulogies poured forth for the ballplayer taken at age 38 when, arguably, his career could've gone on at length. To have called him a humanitarian would have been neither melodramatic nor inappropriate. As Myron Cope said at the time, "Honorary chairman don't die in airplane accidents."

Words of tribute came from all quarters:

Commissioner Bowie Kuhn: "He had a touch of royalty about him. Somehow he transcended super-stardom. His marvelous playing skills rank him among the truly elite. And what a wonderfully good man he was."

Pirate third-string catcher Charlie Sands: "Two weeks after he was gone, I still couldn't believe it. I still expected him to swim ashore someplace."

Pirate manager Bill Virdon: "He was the greatest all-around player of my era."

Singer Bing Crosby, a Pirate stockholder: "He felt the needs of the other fella."

And Puerto Rican schoolboy Roberto Zabala: "He cared enough."

The Washington Post editorialized: "In Pittsburgh, at the empty Three Rivers Stadium, the scoreboard bore the legend, 'Roberto Clemente, 1934–1972.' It might also have read, 'A man of honor played baseball here.'"

Airplane crashes have ended many brilliant athletic careers. In the years following World War Two when commercial airline travel became routine, baseball lost sensational Chicago Cub second-baseman Ken Hubbs, rookie Baltimore catcher Tommy Gastall and, of course, the New York Yankees' all-star catcher Thurman Munson. Legendary Notre Dame coach Knute Rockne died when a small plane crashed in a Kansas wheat field in 1931, and undefeated heavyweight champion Rocky Marciano was killed in a similar accident in 1969.

Entire athletic teams have perished in airplane accidents: 18 U.S. figure skaters in Belgium in 1961; 18 Italian soccer players a dozen years before; the California Polytechnic Institute and the Marshall University football teams almost a decade a part to the day; seven members of the English soccer champion Manchester United.

Pro golfer Tony Lema and middleweight champion Marcel Cerdan were also killed in airplane crashes, and recently one took the lives of most of the Zaire national soccer team.

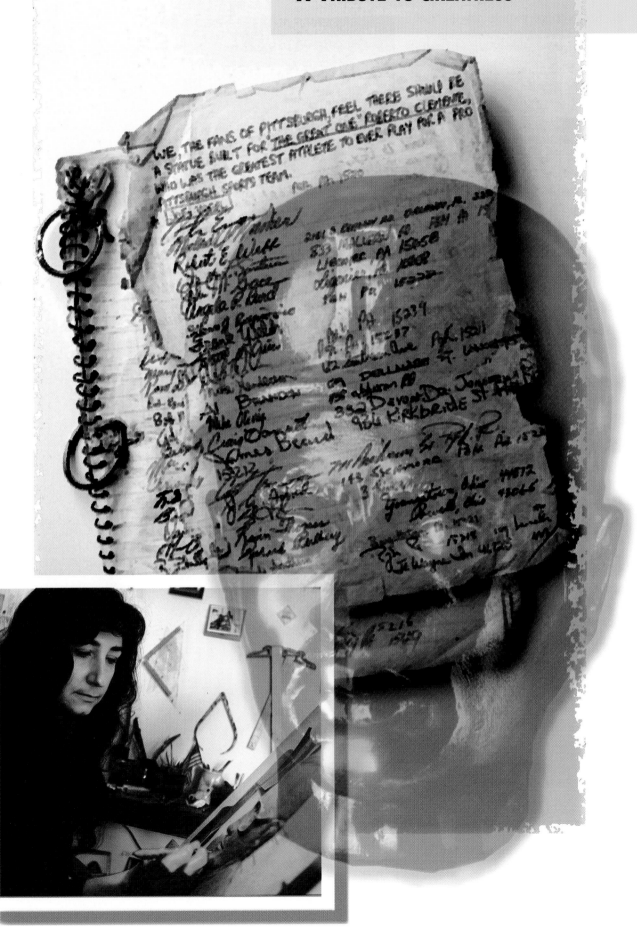

In Susan Wagner's studio near the front windows that allow in the morning light, there is a red-clay bust of a World War Two combat officer… a Native-American in a helmet who is mindful of, oh, George S. Patton or a stern Eisenhower. The face resonates with purpose and resolve; the eyes reflect intelligence; the square jaw appears easily strong enough to break brick.

The bust of the officer, a Colonel, is so real-looking that you want to talk to him. The look of him, and of the other images scattered about, argue that this is the right artist to bring Roberto Clemente to life in bronze.

Across the sunny room in a bookcase, an 18-inch, thickly-muscled black panther slinks along a mahogany shelf, perhaps soon to leap upon several nearby delicate figurines, or rear up and rip paintings and sketches from the surrounding walls. No cat, large or small, would dare mess with the Colonel

There is no order to the room on the third floor of the East Liberty house Susan Wagner and her engineer husband, Richard, have so lovingly restored. The artist's detritus dots this room and a smaller studio leading from it. Drawings, portraits, completed sculptures, graceful figures twisted from wire, small statues . . . they all compete for space with the wherewithal used to create them. At any one moment, Wagner will be working on several projects, artistically alive in many different directions at once. They sit in clumps on the paint-splattered brown floor, awaiting her return.

On this coolish Autumn day, her thoughts are in Beacon, New York, an Adirondack town in the low mountains 80 miles or so North of New York City. In a few days, she will return to the sprawling Tallix Foundry in Beacon to complete her work on a 12-foot statue of Roberto Clemente that will probably be her most important work to date. Months after the fact, she still vividly recalls approaching the task of actual sculpting.

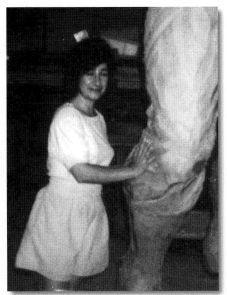

"I walked up to that huge piece of clay . . . and I didn't know where to begin," she says. "I thought, 'who am I to do this? I'm going to get sued! I'll let all of Pittsburgh down.'

"I was so petrified that first day, I couldn't talk."

Actually, her work had begun months before she approached the clay that first day at the foundry. After winning a competition for the commission from the Clemente Statue Fund, she spent "six to nine months, off and on, doing research to develop the concept."

During that time, she studied hundreds of still photographs of Clemente and watched all the film and videotape she could get her hands on. Strangely enough to the layman, Wagner did no preliminary sketching.

The concept settled in her mind, she spent about three weeks sculpting a 15-inch statue and a few days later, had completed a 30-inch version, a maquette.

To describe the process further is to risk confusion: something called a Pantograph machine enlarges the maquette and a steel armature or skeleton is constructed around the enlargement. The skeleton is then surrounded with styrofoam, which is covered with an overlay of thick clay.

"I sculpture that overlay," Wagner explains.

At 5-foot-2, she is less than half the size of her work, so most of her days at the foundry were spent on scaffolds, wearing a safety harness because she tends to keep backing up to get perspective.

The actual sculpting was completed late in the fall and the six-month casting process started, Wagner working with technicians and engineers at Tallix. The New York foundry had to be used because no local facility is large enough.

The casting process involves a plastic mold, removing the clay from the mold, filling it with hot wax—the Lost Wax method—and then finally pouring liquid bronze into the final mold. A couple of weeks before the unveiling July 8 during the week of the All-Star game, a patina coating will be applied to add color and protect the statue.

When the unveiling takes place and the reviews are in, Susan Wagner will take her deepest breath in more than a year.

"When I began the actual sculpting, as I said, I was petrified," Wagner says, "but I thought, 'Well, it's either do this or move to another country.'"

Wagner will not have to relocate. Those who saw her work in its various stages tended to describe it with the same word: breath-taking.

"Working on it, I knew I would let everyone down if it wasn't good," she says. "That's tremendous pressure for an artist. I thought 'you better do this right.' And I'd never done anything that large. But a friend of mine said, 'Susan, no one has done anything that large.'

"It wasn't until the last couple of weeks that I felt comfortable working on it."

Is she happy with the sculpture?

"Yeah, I really do like it," Wagner says, "but I'm apprehensive about people accepting it. And it's going to be there for years and years."

21

Susan Wagner had never seen a baseball game before she was chosen to create the Roberto Clemente statue that will sit at Gate A at Three Rivers Stadium.

"I hadn't when I got the commission," she says. "But I always wanted to do his face. It was beautiful and I could see the intensity in his eyes."

Wagner can't remember when she wasn't an artist.

"All my life," she says. "Art was always a part of my schooling."

The 41-year-old Wagner is a Springdale native; a graduate of Penn Hills High School; spent two years at the Ivy School of Art, and graduated from the University of Pittsburgh in 1981 with a fine arts degree. And with few prospects.

"I couldn't find a job," says Wagner, who turned to the arts after an unsuccessful stint as a secretary who failed to fully master the word processor. "I was a failure."

Not for long. With encouragement from her husband—"He said, 'You want to be a what?'"—Wagner began a freelance career in several artistic mediums.

"Someone saw my sculptures and Matthews, Inc. commissioned me to do some portraits," she says. "Gradually I got a reputation for being dependable and that brought in sculpture work."

In recent years the majority of her work has been bas relief. She has done the busts of every Hall of Fame inductee since 1984 and sculpted the critically-acclaimed Gulf War Memorial in Greensburg.

Currently, Wagner is at work on a variety of projects.

The look that always lives in Steve Blass' eyes suggests a collision between Dennis the Menace and Bambi. The meeting of puckish humor and vulnerability; of accepting the world with amusement and desperately wishing in the heart that it was different.

In 10 summers in the place they call The Show, Blass won 103 games. Through a five-year stretch, he won 78 and was one of the National League's premier pitchers. After the losses, even the bitterest to accept, he was what baseball writers call a stand-up guy. Which meant he didn't skulk and sulk in the players' lounge or take deadline-killing showers, but rather answered their questions with good humor before slipping away to privately chew on his soul. This is not as commonplace as you might think and bespeaks a certain courage of spirit.

Born with lesser athletic gifts, Blass might've become baseball's first real poet: He is that much of a romantic and sensitive enough to separate the game's soldiers from its Roberto Clementes.

The strange course of Blass' career has been well-charted, perhaps overly

so. One season he was a dominant pitcher; the next he could not have hit the water from a rowboat, his control inexplicably shot. Quickly and prematurely, he was gone from the game. The cause remains to this day as arguably baseball's greatest all-time mystery. It is one of the game's cruelties that the phenomena came to be known as Steve Blass' Disease.

Blass suffered his trials with wit and good grace. When the Pirates sent him to their Charleston, West Virginia farm club early in 1974 and asked him to pitch in an exhibition game against the parent club, Blass declined.

"It's bad enough hitting guys I don't know," he explained, "without hurting my friends."

On a magazine assignment, I covered the last game he won in organized baseball, an untidy affair in which he walked 10 or so, hit a few batters and survived through the good offices of the double play. Afterwards, we drank—Blass stayed relatively sober, I didn't—with some players from the Tidewater Braves. One of them said of Blass' painful struggle to regain control of his pitches and thus his career, "There isn't a classier guy in the game." So he remains.

Currently a member of the Pirate broadcast team, Blass specializes in humor and insight; sometimes both in the same instant. Perhaps no former teammate of Clemente's is better-credentialed to talk about him than Blass, who spoke eloquently at his funeral.

On a recent winter morning, Steve Blass worries the subject around his mind over a cup of coffee in a South Hills restaurant. About Clemente, he wants to be precise.

"As the time has passed, he's been lionized," Blass says. "But as a teammate you don't have the same perspective you do years later."

That is prologue: Blass warming up, if you will.

"He was different… he wasn't like the rest of us," Blass goes on. "He took professionalism to a higher degree. After a game, we all wanted to go out for a beer. He wouldn't go. He was compelled by baseball.

"He wasn't one of the soldiers… he was a general."

Baseball is a far more cerebral affair than even the most devoted of fans might imagine. Managers and coaches spend hours plotting tactics, dissecting opponents' weaknesses, maximizing every possible advantage. Team computers may sport the occasional tobacco stain, but they get heavy use and some clubs never deviate from The Book they produce: strategies solely the product of opposition tendencies spat out by sophisticated machines.

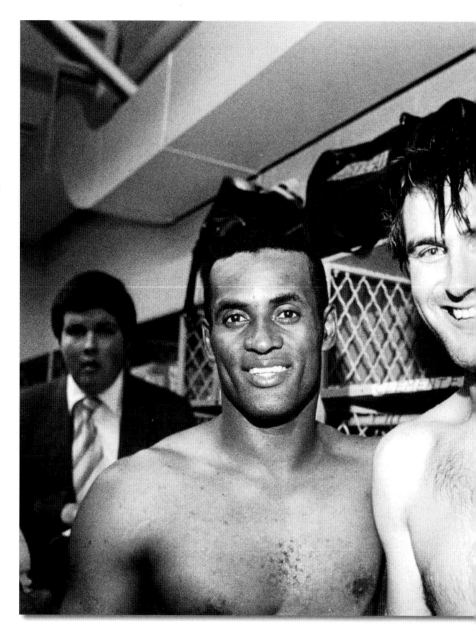

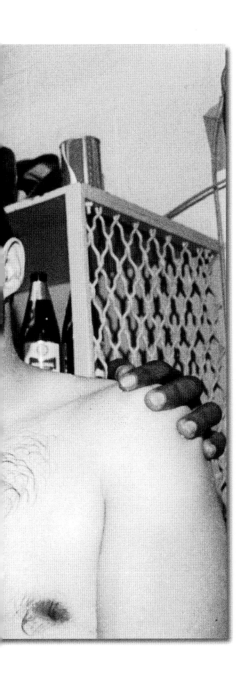

Collectors of Roberto Clemente memorabilia—and there are far more than might be imagined, in Pittsburgh and nationally—have a wealth of new material to consider.

Renewed interest in the Pirate Hall of Famer led to the marketing of new collectibles ranging from a calendar to several limited-edition lithographs.

The calendar (pictured) was produced by John Meiser, the owner of Basic Concepts, and features photographs of Clemente memorabilia, some of it donated by Vera Clemente and never before in circulation.

A likeness of Roberto was available on boxes of Kellogg's Corn Flakes as part of a new marketing program and Sports Impressions has produced a series of Clemente collectibles.

Other new items available include: a limited-edition lithograph by Maser Galleries, a doll by Sports Accessories & Memorabilia, glassware by R & N China Company, and T-shirts produced by OhioPyle Prints.

ROBERTO
1994-1995 BASEBALL CALENDAR. A YEAR TO REMEMBER.
CLEMENTE

Still, the game's action is furious and in moments impossible to choreograph; a spontaneous business that belies its rather silly pastoral image. And so, a generation ago when it was peopled by men who did not carry briefcases and wear Armani and make unspeakable salaries, baseball was viewed as something less than religion by its practitioners.

"To most of us, baseball is a... frivolous game, or some of it is frivolous," Blass says. "It wasn't frivolous to Roberto.

"I can't think of him taking any aspect of the game lightly. His whole essence was on the line once they played the Anthem."

How long Clemente could've sustained that unusual passion for the game is, of course, a matter for conjecture. In his classic poem "To an Athlete Dying Young," A.E. Housman wrote of the virtue of one not outlasting his time:

"Now you will not swell the rout
of lads that wore their honors out,
Runners whom renown outran
and the name died before the man."

Steve Blass likes the poem but, in Clemente's case, is less certain about the sentiment.

"He was 38 when he died, but he had a 25-year old body," Blass says. "He was perfectly proportioned and that would've helped extend his career. Even Mays wasn't built like that... Willie had a heaviness in his chest and shoulders but those skinny legs. The body type would've affected him. Hank Aaron, too."

Expansion that diluted the talent pool would also have lengthened Clemente's career, possibly by years.

"I think he could've played until he was 45 and still been effective," Blass theorizes. "Pitchers were being brought up in that era that weren't ready. Guile alone could've kept him around a long time."

Or pride could've retired Clemente in a heartbeat.

"Yeah, he had his own standards and I'd guess they were pretty high," Blass agrees. "The question is, how would he have judged himself? One thing he couldn't have taken was being embarrassed.

"Being as passionate about the game as he was, and being as aware as he was, he might've been capable of quitting impulsively."

Such speculation, like most, is idle. Yet when greatness is cut short by fate, it is also inevitable. How long would Roberto Clemente have continued to play baseball had his life not ended accidentally? Until he was 40? Even 50? Would injuries have forestalled his career almost overnight? Who knows? What would he have done beyond baseball? Another imponderable, although Blass hazards a guess.

"If he had not been embarrassed, he might've played until he was 50 and still been functional," he says. "I felt he was becoming aware of what he could've been. And he could've become the governor of Puerto Rico.

"He was beginning to understand what sort of future he might have."

21

A feature film on the life of Roberto Clemente is scheduled to go into production later in 1994, according to Arriba Productions.

David Saperstein, creator and script writer of the Academy Award-winning movie "Cocoon," is writing the screenplay. Executive producers for the film will be Micky Hyman, a New York film maker, and sports agent Alicia Berns.

The film is scheduled to be shot in Puerto Rico, Pittsburgh and other U.S. cities.

What follows is mostly for the young; or for those for whom the game of baseball is largely experienced through the prism of recalled youth.

At its best, baseball overwhelms all but the immediate senses. It is most enjoyably consumed through the eyes and the nose and the ears; thinking overmuch about it tends to dull the experience and can be left to the moments when there are no games and thinking is all there is. Then, contemplation has a proper place.

Kids instinctively understand this; at the ball park they do not soil the moment with arguments about free agency and the financial state of the game and the thoughtless greed of the principals. In short, they simply go to the park and leave just enough of the mind at home.

The suggestion here, of course, is to watch as kids do, with a sense of urgency and excitement… an untrammeled anticipation of the what-next of it all. Bring with you an innocence that blurs personal concerns and leaves little in the mind but the simple freedom to enjoy… to exult at your team's successes and experience its failures in your bones. The way kids do. Or a friend of mine, who is a distinguished professor of English at the University of Pittsburgh and a man of sophistication, but who would never consider going to Three Rivers Stadium without wearing his treasured, original St. Louis Browns cap, scuffed and soiled and without which baseball for him loses some of its flavor.

Watch baseball the way Scott Tozzi did, and still struggles to, and the way Danny Bartholomae does and will, hopefully, for some years to come. With joy.

Naturally enough—Tozzi is 42, Danny Bartholomae is 12—they see the game differently. Still, there is a common thread to their experience; both watch through young eyes.

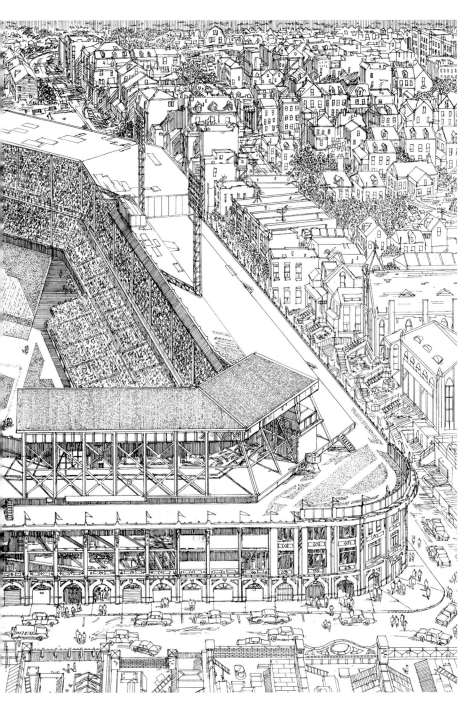

...hing could capture the essence of Forbes Field during Roberto Clemente's career ...e any better than this illustration by Pittsburgh artist Nevin Robinson

Danny did not get to see Roberto Clemente play baseball. That's sort of a shame because he played it a little differently than it's played today. Harder; more intensely. As he once said, "If I smiled more, I would not be as good a player."

Clemente, in fact, played the game with the same sort of innocence that children watch it. Reduced it to the basics. Screened out the peripheral elements.

"When I play right field, I have tunnel vision," he once told Nellie King. "I concentrate so hard, I don't even see anyone else. Then, I relax. I see second base… I see shortstop… finally, I see first base."

"That's a beautiful way to describe it, I think," King says.

At the ball park these days, Scott Tozzi often longs—the word is not too strong, I think—for what was. Going to Forbes Field on a trolley. Hanging around the press gate before the game to see Bob Prince stroll in wearing lime green pants and plaid jackets that blurred the vision and left tiny sparks burning in the viewer's eyes. And, before he got too old for it, having a hero.

"Clemente put right field on the map," Tozzi says flatly, as if Babe Ruth nor Henry Aaron nor Frank Robinson nor anyone else had ever really played the position. "Everything about him was unique. The basket catch… the way he would slide to make a catch… everything."

A successful businessman and lifelong baseball fan, Scott Tozzi probably sees 35 to 40 Pirate games each summer. He played as a kid in the Frick Park Little League where, incidentally, he once ran over a kid at second base who later became a contract killer. Baseball remains a passion; when he goes to the ball park these days, he tries to take a bit of his youth with him.

"That's all you lived for in those days, your Dad saying 'we're going to the game,'" he sighs. "You didn't take your glove off all day. If it rained, you were devastated."

Danny Bartholomae, an inordinately bright kid and the son of educators, sees about as many Pirate games each season as Scott Tozzi. He, too, was a little leaguer, playing "anywhere they put me… second base, third, the outfield."

Like Tozzi, at the ball park Danny seizes the immediate moment and doesn't overly concern himself with corollaries. If there is no sense of nostalgia for him, there is keen awareness that a sense of history is part of the baseball experience. To appreciate the brilliance of Andy Van Slyke running a long drive to earth, Danny understands that it helps to have the sort of context provided by knowing there came before Van Slyke a Roberto Clemente.

What Danny Bartholomae likes best about the game is simply "playing it." But he also reads about it and likes to write about it. Last winter, he did a paper for school on Roberto Clemente. In him, one suspects, is a latent sportswriter.

"I heard a lot about him being an inspiration to people," Danny says.

For Scott Tozzi, Clemente was enough inspiration to become a serious, life-long baseball fan. And one who wishes there were fewer Bonds and more Clementes.

"Most of today's players take," Tozzi muses. "He gave."

Two racehorses were named for Roberto Clemente by former Pirate owner John Galbreath, one of the distinguished horsemen of his generation whose Darby Dan stable produced Kentucky Derby winners Chateaugay and Proud Clarion.

The first horse Galbreath named for Clemente was less distinguished. Campeon Battey (Batting Champion) was, in fact, a waste of good oats and amounted to nothing on the racetrack.

Undaunted, a few years later, Galbreath named one of his thoroughbreds "Roberto." When he did not run well in this country, Roberto the horse was shipped to Great Britain to race. In no particular surprise, although he raced as a distinct longshot that afternoon, Roberto won the famed Epsom Derby, arguably the greatest race in the world.

Aman is only as good as his dream, a poet once observed.

If that is so, there can be little dispute that Roberto Clemente was a good man. His dream—not in any melodramatic sense but a goal he established at length and diligently worked toward realizing—was to build a sports facility for the underprivileged children of Puerto Rico; his death and the manner in which it occurred made that dream a reality.

City of Sport—Ciudad Deportiva—sits on 240 acres of rich, red soil just off the Iturreque Road in the San Juan outskirts, ironically enough just a few miles from the site of Clemente's death.

The government of Puerto Rico donated the land, worth $18 million; baseball fans chipped in more than $500,000, and the Puerto Rican legislature passed a bill that added the necessary $12 million to complete the facility. Finally, the Pirates arranged for a number of two-game exhibition series between major-league teams in Puerto Rico to raise additional funds.

Originally, four baseball diamonds were built around an observation tower and the complex included: two softball fields, a soccer field, a track, an Olympic swimming pool and tennis and basketball courts. In recent years, three baseball diamonds were added. The expanded facility now also includes: four professional tennis courts, four outdoor volleyball courts, three covered basketball courts, a recreational park for children, a track and field stadium, 10 batting cages, and a building that houses an office complex and will be the site of the Roberto Clemente museum. To be completed soon are a large dormitory and a golf driving range.

A dream—Roberto Clemente's Ciudad Deportiva—begins to take shape

Every year, from June through August, 2600 kids spend two weeks at Ciudad Deportiva and since it opened, it has accommodated more than 100,000 children and visitors. It also operates after-school programs for under-privileged kids from six to 14 and social service programs including Head Start.

What Roberto Clemente had in mind—a place to serve as a respite for and an inspiration to the poor children of his country—has been achieved.

Make no mistake. These kids come from a grinding poverty matched few places in the world. The slum barrios of Puerto Rico are the equal of any in terms of inadequate food and shelter, rampant disease, and hopelessness. The idea at Ciudad Deportiva was, and is, to instill a measure of hope for the future.

"The people still talk about Roberto," said former City of Sport executive director Jose Seda. "There are very few men who would do what he was doing the day he died. He had a great love for people."

The complex needs about $100,000 a year to operate and Vera Clemente serves as executive director and donates most of her time to the project.

"Roberto hoped the project would be a way of bringing children and parents together, too," she said.

Signed First Contract
1952

1954
Montreal

Named National League
Most Valuable Player
1966
Sporting News
Player of the Year
1966

197

Roberto Clemente
1934–1972

12 Gold Glove Awards From 1961–1972

Series-winning Home Run

1971 World Series MVP

385

World Series Record
Hit Safely in Every Game
1960 & 1971

3,000 th Hit
September 30, 1972

Lifetime Batting
Average .317

For years, Clemente, who believed strongly in the socially-redeeming value of sport, saw not one but many sports cities as his legacy.

"I will work with children; that will keep me in the game forever," he said once when asked the cliché question about what he would do when he retired from baseball. "I'd like to work with kids all the time, if I live long enough.

"This is my dream. I don't know exactly what this Sports City will be like . . . but it will be beautiful. It will be open to everybody, no matter who they are.

"After I open the first one in Puerto Rico, I will open others. I will do this thing because that is what God meant me to do.

"Baseball is just something that gave me a chance to do this."

It is reasonable to suggest that if any man can be said to be pleased with his legacy, Roberto Clemente would have been. In his homeland, all these years after his death, he remains a mythic figure. His wife carries on his work; his sons have grown to be fine men. And he seems to have been prescient, once saying, "I'd like to be remembered as the type of ballplayer I was."

He is. And it is altogether fitting to add that for a single generation, no one played the enduring game of baseball with more fire and grace and heart.

Clemente and her sons, Roberto, Jr., (standing), Enrique (lower left) and Luis

TO ORDER THIS BOOK

Telephone: **1-800-333-1636** or, in the Pittsburgh area, **(412) 433-6666**.

CREDITS

Reflections on Roberto was designed by *Jeffrey Boyd* who also supervised the production; *Mark Hobson* created all of the chapter title pages (including the front cover), and photographed all of the Clemente memorabilia; *Mike Malle* created the illustration on pages 124/125 depicting highlights of Roberto's career; *Grant Paul Design, Inc.,* was responsible for pre-press and print production; Composite film was output by *Image&Ink*; and *Geyer Printing Company, Inc.,* printed the book. Thanks also go to Sally Pennline and Linda Scharf for editorial and production help.

PHOTO CREDITS

The majority of sports photography during most of Roberto Clemente's career was produced by and for newspapers, not the slick glossy color magazines of today. The archiving and crediting of photos was left to the wire services and newspapers with varying degrees of success. Copyrights and attributions didn't seem as important in the 50's and 60's as they are today, so many photos from that era have simply become impossible to identify. All of which is to say that we have made every reasonable effort to credit the both the photographer and the copyright holders and sincerely apologize to anyone not properly credited.

The credits are listed by "spread", that is two side-by-side pages. When a page number is given (i.e. 24) it means 24 and 25 together. Photos are listed in clockwise rotation beginning with the upper left photo. "n/a" indicates that no credit or source was available, or that the photo is public domain. Our thanks to all who helped in the search…

Page 2: National Baseball League; UPI/BETTMAN; n/a. Page 4: Pittsburgh Pirates; Mark Hobson. Page 6: UPI/BETTMANN; New York *Herald Tribune.* Page 8; Pittsburgh Pirates. Page 10: Darryl Norenberg; n/a; AP. Page 12: AP; n/a;Pittsburgh Pirates; UPI/BETTMANN. Page 14: National Baseball Library and Archive, Cooperstown, NY; Pittsburgh Pirates; National Baseball League; n/a. Page 16: Tom Mosser. Page 18: UPI/BETTMANN; UPI/BETTMANN; UPI/BETTMANN. Page 20: Chicago *Sun-Times;* Pittsburgh Pirates; Pittsburgh Pirates.Page 22: UPI/BETTMANN. Page 24: UPI/BETTMANN. Page 26: Luis Mayoral; Pittsburgh Pirates; AP. Page 28: Pittsburgh Pirates. Page 30: n/a; AP; AP; AP. Page 32: Ed Morgan. Page 34: UPI/BETTMANN; AP; National Baseball Library and Archive, Cooperstown, NY. Page 36: n/a. Page 38: Luis Mayoral. Page 40: n/a. Page 42:

National Baseball Library and Archive, Cooperstown, NY; National Baseball Library and Archive, Cooperstown, NY; Luis Mayoral. Page 44: National Baseball Library and Archive, Cooperstown, NY. Page 46: UPI/BETTMANN. Page 48: National Baseball Library and Archive, Cooperstown, NY; Luis Mayoral; Luis Mayoral. Page 50: Pittsburgh Pirates. Page 52: Pittsburgh Pirates. Page 54: Luis Mayoral; Luis Mayoral; National Baseball Library and Archive, Cooperstown, NY. Page 56: Pittsburgh Pirates; Pittsburgh Pirates. Page 58: Pittsburgh Pirates. Page 60: Tom Mosser. Page 62: Pittsburgh Pirates; Pittsburgh Pirates; Pittsburgh Pirates; UPI/BETTMANN. Page 64: UPI/BETTMANN; Pittsburgh Pirates; Pittsburgh Pirates. Page 66: Pittsburgh Pirates; Pittsburgh Pirates. Page 68: Pittsburgh Pirates. Page 70: UPI/BETTMANN. Page 72: Pittsburgh Pirates. Page 74: AP; Pittsburgh Pirates; Pittsburgh Pirates. Page 76: Pittsburgh Pirates. Page 78: Pittsburgh Pirates. Page 80: Pittsburgh Pirates; Pittsburgh

Pirates; AP. Page 82: AP; Pittsburgh Pirates; Pittsburgh Pirates. Page 84: Pittsburgh Pirates. Page 86: UPI/BETTMANN; Pittsburgh Pirates; AP. Page 88: Pittsburgh Pirates. Page 90: Pittsburgh Pirates. Page 92: Bob Smizik. Page 94: Pittsburgh Pirates; Pittsburgh Pirates; *El Dia* Newspaper. Page 96: n/a. Page 98: AP; AP. Page 100: Luis Mayoral; Pittsburgh Pirates; AP; UPI/BETTMANN; Chicago *Sun Times.* Page 102: UPI/BETTMANN; UPI/BETTMANN; AP; UPI/BETTMANN. Page 104: Pittsburgh Pirates. Page 106: Mark Hobson; Susan Wagne, Susan Wagner. Page 108: Mark Hobson. Page 110: Pittsburgh Pirates. Page 112: UPI/BETTMANN; Page 114: Pittsburgh Pirates; UPI/BETTMANN. Page 116: National Baseball League. Page 118: Nevin Robinson. Page 122: n/a; Pittsburgh Pirates; Pittsburgh Pirates; Pittsburgh Pirates. Page 124: Mike Malle. Page 126: Pittsburgh Pirates. Inside Back Cover: Mark Hobson/Jeff Boyd. Outside Back Cover: Pittsburgh Pirates.

Mostly, they were bought for the bubble gum that came in the package with them, and clung to them with a lover's grip so that when separated, you got some ink on your gum or a damaged card that showed, say, Mickey Mantle without his nose.

They weren't collected, not in any meaningful sense, but rather stacked and gathered by rubber band. Or, as we say around here, and nowhere else, gum band.

Nobody thought about them 35 years ago as valuable, although the card of a favorite player was regarded as more precious than, oh, a sister. And instead of being encased in some sort of protective envelope, they were carried in a hip pocket against that moment when some kid said, "Hey, wanna' flip?'"

No, the baseball cards of a generation ago were not collected, perhaps decades later to pay for a retirement, but flipped and soon tattered beyond recognition. Collecting is more valuable, of course; flipping was more fun.

The Clemente cards pictured to the right have been preserved by Clemente memorabilia guru Joe Vogel of Carrick. He has every last one ever produced—none of which has ever spun in the breeze of a Spring morning and fallen lightly on a concrete sidewalk or backyard grass.

Strangely enough, the early cards refer to Clemente as "Bob." In time, the good people at Topps recognized the grievous error. Roberto Clemente was never a Bob. Or Bobby. Or even Robby, which was what Bob Prince called him and which, at first, made Clemente's eyes squint in exasperation.

No, he was Roberto, or to some in his family, "Momen." Still, his baseball cards are valuable, not only monetarily but because a close examination of them is one way to trace his 18-year career. Signed and in, as they say, mint condition, they are worth serious money.

Just don't flip them.